PERSONAL FINANCE FOR TEENS

A ROADMAP FROM ALLOWANCE TO INVESTMENT AS YOU OPTIMIZE MONEY SKILLS, SAFELY SAVE, SPEND AND BUDGET TO BUILD WEALTH AND PREPARE FOR A PROSPEROUS FUTURE

A. P. MCMILLAN

TABLE OF CONTENTS

Introduction   7

1. UNDERSTANDING PERSONAL FINANCE BASICS   9
    1.1 Decoding Financial Jargon: A Teen's Glossary   9
    1.2 The Art of Budgeting: Creating Your First
    Budget   12
    1.3 Smart Saving Strategies for Your First Bank
    Account   14
    1.4 Basic Principles of Money Management: From
    Allowance to Income   16
    1.5 Understanding Banks: What They Can Do
    for You   18

2. EARNING AND MANAGING YOUR MONEY   23
    2.1 Exploring Part-Time Jobs and What They Can
    Offer   23
    2.2 Side Hustles for Teens: Turning Passions into
    Paychecks   26
    2.3 Understanding Your Paycheck: Taxes and
    Deductions Explained   28
    2.4 Financial Responsibility: Handling Your Money
    with Care   31

3. SPENDING WISELY   35
    3.1 Needs vs. Wants: A Guide to Smart Spending   35
    3.2 Emotional Spending   38
    3.3 Online Shopping Smart: Avoiding Traps and
    Scams   40
    3.4 The True Cost of Peer Pressure: Keeping Up vs.
    Catching Up   43
    3.5 Bargain Hunting: Tips for Finding the Best in
    Deals   45

4. SAVING AND INVESTING FOR THE FUTURE   49

   4.1 Why Start Saving Early: The Magic of Compound Interest   49

   4.2 Introduction to Investing: Stocks, Bonds, ETFs, and Mutual Funds   52

   4.3 Understanding Return on Investment (ROI)   54

   4.4 Using Digital Tools to Boost Your Savings   56

   4.5 Retirement Accounts for Teens: It's Never Too Early to Plan   59

5. USING CREDIT WISELY   63

   5.1 The ABCs of Credit Cards: What Every Teen Needs to Know   63

   5.2 Building and Maintaining a Healthy Credit Score   66

   5.3 The Dangers of Debt: How to Use Credit Safely   68

   5.4 Student Loans: What You Should Know Before Borrowing   70

6. ADVANCED MONEY MANAGEMENT TECHNIQUES   75

   6.1 Advanced Budgeting: Planning for Big Purchases   75

   6.2 Financial Forecasting: Predicting Your Money's Future   78

   6.3 Wealth Building Strategies for Teens   80

   6.4 Managing Money Across Different Platforms   82

7. FINANCIAL PLANNING FOR SIGNIFICANT EXPENSES   89

   7.1 Saving for College: A Step-by-Step Guide   89

   7.2 Buying Your First Car: Financial Tips and Tricks   92

   7.3 Planning for Study Abroad: Budgeting for the Big Trip   94

   7.4 Emergency Funds: Why and How to Start One   96

8. PROTECTING YOURSELF FINANCIALLY   101

   8.1 Identifying and Avoiding Scams Targeted at Teens   101

   8.2 Insurance Basics: What Teens Need to Know   104

   8.3 Safeguarding Your Online Banking   106

   8.4 Intellectual Property and Money: Protecting Your Creations   109

9. NAVIGATING THE DIGITAL FINANCIAL WORLD — 113
9.1 Mastering Online Banking: Tips and Tricks — 113
9.2 Cryptocurrency: Basics for Teens — 116
Risks and Rewards — 117
Getting Started Safely — 118
9.3 Financial Apps: What's Available for Teens? — 119
9.4 The Role of Social Media in Financial Decisions — 121

10. ETHICAL AND RESPONSIBLE FINANCE — 125
10.1 Socially Responsible Investing: Making Money While Doing Good — 125
10.2 The Impact of Your Financial Decisions on the Environment — 128
10.3 Ethical Shopping: How Your Purchases Affect Others — 131
10.4 Supporting Causes Through Financial Choices — 133

11. PREPARING FOR FINANCIAL INDEPENDENCE — 137
11.1 From Teen to Adult: Steps Toward Financial Independence — 137
11.2 Negotiating Salaries and Benefits for Your First Job — 140
11.3 Moving Out: Budgeting for Your First Place — 142
11.4 Long-Term Financial Planning: Setting Life Goals — 145

12. STAYING MOTIVATED AND FINANCIALLY INFORMED — 149
12.1 Keeping Up with Financial News Without Getting Overwhelmed — 149
12.2 Financial Podcasts and Books Every Teen Should Know About — 152
12.3 Joining Financially Minded Communities — 154
12.4 Setting and Reviewing Financial Goals as You Grow — 156

Conclusion — 161
References — 165

Did you know that less than half of high school students in the U.S. are required to take a course on personal finance? It's a sad statistic, especially considering how crucial financial skills are to navigating life successfully. This gap in our education system is what drives me to reach out to you directly through this book.

Your journey can start with saving small change from your weekly allowance or part-time job and evolve into managing budgets and investments. Through these financial habits, you will discover the power and freedom that come with understanding money. I want you to experience this freedom. That's why I wrote this book—to give you the tools and knowledge to take control of your financial future, starting now.

"Personal Finance for Teens" isn't just another dry textbook. It's a roadmap designed specifically for you, a teen ready to navigate the exciting world of money. This book breaks down complex financial concepts into manageable, bite-sized pieces. I'll cover everything from setting up your first savings account to understanding the real magic behind compound interest. Each chapter builds on the last, transforming you from a beginner into a savvy financial navigator.

Why focus on personal finance during your teen years? Starting early can make a profound difference. It's about setting positive habits and avoiding common pitfalls like credit card debt. It's also about seizing opportunities, whether that's investing early or starting a business. With each page, you'll learn not just how to save, but how to grow your money wisely.

As we dive into these pages together, remember, this book is for you—regardless of where you're starting. Whether you're a complete novice or you have some savings already, there's something here to enhance your understanding and confidence. I've packed this guide with real-life examples, actionable advice, and stories of young people, just like you, who have mastered their personal finance.

So, are you ready to take charge of your financial destiny? Let's do this together. Flip the page, and let's start this journey toward a prosperous and independent financial future. Remember, your path to financial literacy begins now. This book is here to guide you every step of the way. Let's get started and unlock the potential of your personal finance!

CHAPTER ONE

UNDERSTANDING PERSONAL FINANCE BASICS

Have you ever felt like the world of money is a giant puzzle, where everyone but you seem to know how to fit the pieces together? You're not alone. Many teens (and even adults) feel out of the loop when it comes to managing money, often because no one has taken the time to translate the confusing jargon into simple language they can understand. This chapter is your starting point in this journey toward becoming financially fluent. We'll break down those baffling terms, use analogies that make sense, and even play with interactive tools that will turn your learning into an adventure.

1.1 DECODING FINANCIAL JARGON: A TEEN'S GLOSSARY

Understanding Common Terms

Let's start by demystifying some basic terms you've probably heard but may not fully understand. Terms like 'interest', 'debt', 'assets', and 'liabilities' are not just for bankers or investors; they are part of everyday financial decisions.

- Interest: Think of interest as the price you pay for using someone else's money or the reward you get for letting others use yours. If you borrow money to buy a new bike, the interest is what you pay extra to the lender. Conversely, if you save money in a bank, the interest is what the bank pays you for keeping your money there.
- Debt: Simply put, debt is money that you owe. Whether it's a few dollars borrowed from a friend to cover lunch or a loan from a bank to buy a car, it's debt. It's like a financial promise you make to pay back what you borrowed, often with interest.
- Assets: These are things you own that have value. Your assets could include the cash in your wallet, the savings account in your name, or even a vintage comic book collection. Assets are your financial treasures.
- Liabilities: On the other side, liabilities are what you owe. Think of them as the opposite of assets. Your debts are liabilities because they represent money you need to pay back.

Everyday Analogies

To make these terms stick, let's relate them to something you're familiar with—video games. Imagine you're playing a game where you start with some assets (coins, tools, powers). As you progress, you invest these assets to gain more advanced tools and powers (this is your investment growing through interest). But, if you borrow resources from a teammate (incur debt), you owe them back, potentially with a bonus (interest on the debt) for helping you out.

Interactive Game Feature

Now that you have been introduced to these terms, dive into the interactive game on the Practical Money Skills website (https://www.practicalmoneyskills.com/en/play/payoff.html). Here, you'll find clear definitions and play an exciting game where you help two teens manage their money as they gear up for a video competition. It's a fun and engaging way to boost your financial know-how. These two will be put through a series of crisis scenarios, and it is up to you to help them make smart financial decisions to complete their video on time. It's a hands-on way to ensure you understand these concepts inside and out.

Encourage Exploration

Now, I encourage you to start spotting these terms in your daily life. Maybe you hear about interest rates on the news, or your parents discuss balancing their assets and liabilities at the end of the month. Whenever you come across a financial term, try to connect it with the definitions and examples you've learned here. The more you practice, the more natural these concepts will become, making you confident in financial discussions. You can also explore additional resources listed below that I have found helpful while researching, conveniently categorized based on your interests.

Gaming Tools

- Financial Football – Games - https://www.financialfootball.com/
- Financial Soccer – Games - https://financialsoccer.com/en

Family Tools

- FamZoo – https://famzoo.com/
- iAllowance app (Apple)– allowance (can be based on chores and/or auto-deposit) https://www.jumpgapsoftware.com/allowance/index.html
- Chores & Allowance Bot app (Android) - https://wingboat.com/AllowanceBot/index.html
- RoosterMoney (U.K. only) - https://roostermoney.com/

Educational Tools

- World of Money – "Moguls" level - https://www.worldofmoney.org/
- Step banking – https://step.com/
- Banzai - https://banzai.org/courses/finlit/middle-school
- Greenlight - https://greenlight.com/teens
- Washington State Department of Financial Institutions. Financial education at home: Grades 9-12 - https://dfi.wa.gov/financial-education/at-home/grades-9-12

1.2 THE ART OF BUDGETING: CREATING YOUR FIRST BUDGET

Imagine you've just received your allowance, maybe some extra cash from a birthday, or earnings from a part-time job. It feels great to have money in your pocket, right? Now, let's talk about how to manage that money wisely through budgeting. Budgeting might sound like a chore, but it's really about making sure you have enough money for the things you need and the things you want, both now and in the future. Let's walk through how to create your first budget, step by step.

First, gather all your sources of income. This could be your weekly or monthly allowance, money from odd jobs like babysitting or lawn mowing, or maybe a stipend from a part-time job. Once you have a clear picture of your earnings, it's time to track where your money goes. Start by listing all your typical expenses. This might include money you spend on snacks after school, monthly subscriptions (like gaming services or mobile apps), and amounts you save for bigger goals like a new game console or concert tickets. At this point, just jotting down these figures on a piece of paper or a simple spreadsheet can be incredibly eye-opening.

Now, let's dive deeper into categorizing these expenses. Split them into 'needs' and 'wants.' 'Needs' are expenses that are essential for your everyday living, like transportation costs or school supplies. 'Wants' are things that you would like to have but can live without, like eating out with friends or a new outfit. Further, categorize your expenses as 'fixed' or 'variable.' Fixed expenses are those that don't change much from month to month, like subscription fees. Variable expenses can fluctuate, like spending money on outings. Why categorize? It helps you identify areas where you can adjust your spending more easily. Understanding where your money goes each month is the first step toward making informed decisions about controlling your spending.

Consider using a budgeting tool or app to keep your budget organized and easy to manage. There are many free resources available that are designed specifically for beginners. These tools often provide templates where you can simply input your income and expenses, and they do the math for you. They can also help you set up notifications for due payments or alert you when you're nearing your spending limit in a certain category, which can be especially helpful for staying on track.

Let's put this into a real-life scenario. Suppose you want to buy a new smartphone in six months, and it costs $600. You figure out that you need to save $100 each month to buy it without touching other savings or incurring debt. Start by looking at your variable expenses to see where you can cut back. Perhaps you could skip buying two coffees a week and save around $30 a month. Maybe consider cutting back on one subscription service or buying fewer in-game items. Adjusting your budget to accommodate your savings goal can help ensure you reach it without drastically altering your lifestyle.

Creating and sticking to a budget doesn't just help you manage your money more effectively; it empowers you to make financial decisions that can bring you closer to your dreams, whether that's owning the latest tech gadget, going to a dream concert, or just feeling secure in your financial future. By starting this practice early in life, you're setting yourself up for a lifetime of financial awareness and responsibility, turning what might seem like constraints into a launchpad for achieving your goals.

1.3 SMART SAVING STRATEGIES FOR YOUR FIRST BANK ACCOUNT

When it comes to managing your money, opening your first bank account is a bit like stepping onto the field for your first big game. You're excited, maybe a little nervous, and ready to play your best. But just like in sports, having the right equipment—in this case, the right type of bank account—can make all the difference in how well you perform. Let's explore how to choose an account that holds your money and helps it grow.

For starters, look for accounts that are friendly to young savers like you. Many banks offer student or youth accounts that come with perks such as no minimum balance requirements, no monthly fees, and even some rewards for good grades or regular deposits. These features are crucial because they help you keep your money working for you rather than paying fees. Also, consider the interest rates offered. While rates on savings accounts are generally low across the board these days, even a small difference can add up over time. Choosing a bank that offers a competitive interest rate can give your savings a nice boost without any extra effort on your part.

Now, let's talk about one of the most exciting parts of saving: compound interest. Imagine you're planting a tree. Each dollar you save is like a seed you plant. Over time, not only does the seed grow into a tree, but it also starts producing more seeds, which in turn grow into more trees. That's compound interest—earning interest on your interest. For example, if you start with $100 in a savings account with a 2% annual interest rate, compounded yearly, you'll have about $102 after the first year. In the second year, you'll earn interest on that $102, not just the original $100, meaning you'll end up with about $104.04, and so on. Over many years, that growth accelerates without you having to do a thing.

Setting savings goals is your next step. It's essential to be specific about what you're saving for because it gives you a clear target and helps keep you motivated. Maybe you're saving for a new laptop, a car, or even starting to stash away cash for college. Whatever your goals, break them down into manageable steps. If that laptop costs $1,000 and you want to buy it in a year, you need to save about $83 a month. Keep track of your progress monthly, and adjust as needed. This not only teaches you the discipline needed to save but also gives you real-world skills in budgeting and planning.

Lastly, let's make saving a bit more fun and a lot less of a chore. Technology can be a huge ally here. Many banks now offer features that automatically transfer your change to a savings account every time you make a purchase. For instance, if you buy a coffee for $2.75, these tools can round up the cost to $3.00 and put the $0.25 into your savings. It might not seem like much, but these small amounts can grow significantly over time, just like with compound interest. Another fun tool is setting up automatic transfers to your savings account right after you get your allowance or pay from a job. Think of it as paying your future self first. It's a habit that can set you up for lifelong financial stability.

By starting with the proper account, understanding the magic of compound interest, setting clear goals, and using tools that make saving effortless, you're laying down a strong foundation for your financial future. Remember, each small step you take today is a leap toward your bigger dreams of tomorrow.

1.4 BASIC PRINCIPLES OF MONEY MANAGEMENT: FROM ALLOWANCE TO INCOME

Understanding how money flows in and out of your hands might seem straightforward, but it's actually where many stumble, even adults. Think of your financial life as a water tank, where the water level should ideally continuously rise or at least steady. The water flowing in represents your income, while the water flowing out represents your expenses. The goal is to ensure that more water is coming in than going out. This simple concept of cash flow is foundational to managing your finances effectively.

Let's say you earn money from different sources — perhaps a regular allowance, some cash from babysitting, and occasional birthday bonuses from relatives. This income fills up your tank. Then there are expenses, everything from necessary school supplies to outings with friends. Each expense drains some water from your tank. The key to managing your cash flow positively is ensuring your tank doesn't run dry — essentially, you should aim to spend less than you earn. This might mean making tough choices, like maybe deciding against a trendy purchase or opting for a less expensive outing with friends to ensure your tank stays healthy.

Managing irregular income can be particularly tricky. Suppose you're working seasonal jobs or earning money from gigs like tutoring during the school year. In that case, the flow into your tank can be uneven — a lot coming in at one time, and then perhaps little to none at other times. Consider setting aside part of the large inflows into a savings account to smooth out these highs and lows. Think of it as a buffer zone. This way, you can draw from it during the leaner months, keeping your water level more consistent. This method requires discipline and planning, but is training for future financial stability. It's about creating a cushion that helps you confidently handle money, ensuring you're covered when the gigs dry up.

Moreover, earning your first significant income, whether from a part-time job or a larger allowance, can feel incredibly empowering. However, it also tests your responsibility. It can be tempting to spend impulsively, especially when you suddenly have more money at your disposal than ever before. This is where you need to pause and think about the long-term benefits rather than just immediate gratification. For instance, saving a portion of your income from a summer job could go towards college expenses, reducing future debt. Or, it could fund an entrepreneurial project you've been contemplating. Every dollar you don't spend now is a dollar that can grow, through savings or investments, and contribute to your financial security down the road.

Handling money responsibly from the start sets a powerful precedent for your financial future. It's not just about saving; it's about developing a mindset that values foresight, self-control, and the ability to plan ahead. These are the qualities that distinguish those who are just getting by from those who are truly in control of their financial destinies. Remember, every decision you make about money today shapes the landscape of your tomorrow. So, each time you earn, think of how best to use that money to serve your present needs and future aspirations.

1.5 UNDERSTANDING BANKS: WHAT THEY CAN DO FOR YOU

Navigating the banking world might seem like a daunting task, especially when you're just starting to take control of your financial life. However, understanding what banks offer and how they operate can significantly empower you, enhancing your ability to manage money efficiently. Let's explore how to choose the right bank, open and manage accounts, utilize bank services effectively, and ensure your financial security with proper safety measures.

Choosing the Right Bank

When it comes to selecting a bank, think of it as choosing a new smartphone: you want one that meets your needs, is reliable, and doesn't come with unnecessary costs. Banks and credit unions both offer places to save your money, but they operate a bit differently. Banks are for-profit institutions, typically offering a wider range of services and more extensive online and mobile banking technologies. Credit unions, on the other hand, are nonprofit and owned by their members, often resulting in lower fees and higher interest rates on savings accounts.

When choosing between them, consider what's more important to you. A credit union might be your best bet if you're looking for higher interest rates and lower fees. However, a traditional bank might be more suitable if you prefer robust online banking tools and widespread ATM access. Always look at the fee structure—monthly maintenance fees, ATM fees, and overdraft charges should be significant considerations. Also, assess the accessibility of physical branches and ATMs, customer service quality, and any additional services that could benefit you, like mobile deposit capabilities or financial education resources.

How to Open and Manage a Bank Account

Opening your first bank account is a major step in your financial journey. To start, you'll need a few key documents: a government-issued I.D. (like a passport or a driver's license), a Social Security number, proof of address (such as a utility bill or a school report card), and sometimes a minimum deposit. The process can typically be done online or in person at a branch. If you're under 18, you'll likely need a parent or guardian to open a joint account with you, which they can oversee until you come of age.

Once your account is open, managing it effectively is crucial. Keep track of your balance regularly to avoid overdrafts, which can incur hefty fees. Most banks offer online and mobile banking tools that allow you to monitor your account, set up automatic payments for recurring bills, and transfer money between accounts. These tools can help you maintain a clear picture of your financial status at all times, ensuring you can react quickly to any issues or opportunities.

Understanding Bank Services

Banks offer a wide array of services that can be incredibly beneficial, especially as your financial needs grow. Beyond basic checking and savings accounts, many banks provide bill pay services, which can help you manage monthly expenses without the hassle of mailing checks. Mobile banking apps have become particularly valuable, offering features like depositing checks through your smartphone and setting up real-time alerts for transactions, which keep you informed and protect against fraudulent activity.

Learning to use ATMs safely is another crucial skill. Always be aware of your surroundings when making transactions at an ATM. Use machines in well-lit, secure areas, and shield the keypad when entering your PIN to protect your account information. Remember, while ATMs are incredibly convenient for withdrawing cash, depositing money, and checking account balances, they can also be a target for fraudsters, so vigilance is key.

Safety and Security Tips

In today's digital world, securing your financial information is more important than ever. Always use strong, unique passwords for online banking accounts and change them regularly. Be wary of phishing scams—fraudulent emails, texts, or calls that try to trick you into giving away personal information. Always verify the contact by calling your bank directly using a number from their official website if you suspect any communication might be a scam. Additionally, take advantage of any additional security features your bank offers, such as two-factor authentication, which provides an extra layer of security beyond just your password.

Furthermore, be mindful of your privacy settings on any financial apps. Ensure that your sensitive information is protected by understanding what data the app collects and how it is used. Many apps will offer privacy settings that allow you to control the sharing of your data; make sure these are configured to provide maximum security.

Understanding these aspects of banking can dramatically increase your financial literacy and confidence. By choosing the right bank, making informed decisions about account management, utilizing available services to their fullest potential, and prioritizing security, you set the stage for a solid financial future, equipped to handle the opportunities and challenges that may come your way.

CHAPTER TWO

EARNING AND MANAGING YOUR MONEY

Imagine you're standing at the threshold of a vast maze that twists and turns through the landscape of earning and managing money. It's a place where each path could lead to new opportunities and learning experiences. While this might seem daunting at first, navigating it can be exciting, especially when you know you're not just working to earn but also to learn and grow. In this chapter, we'll explore the multifaceted world of part-time jobs—uncovering not just the financial benefits, but also the personal and professional growth that accompanies these experiences.

2.1 EXPLORING PART-TIME JOBS AND WHAT THEY CAN OFFER

Identify Opportunities

Finding the right part-time job can sometimes feel like searching for a needle in a haystack. It's not just about what pays; it's about what fits. Start by considering your interests and how they might align with available job opportunities. Are you passionate about technology? Perhaps a job at a local electronics store could be a match. Love being outdoors? Maybe a garden center or recreational facility position could be perfect for you. Utilize job boards like Indeed, Glassdoor, and even specific youth job portals that filter opportunities suitable for teens. Don't overlook the value of your local community centers and libraries, which often have bulletin boards with job postings that might not be listed online. Social media platforms can also be an opportunity—many local businesses post job openings on their profiles.

Benefits Beyond Money

The perks of part-time jobs extend far beyond the paycheck. These early work experiences are fertile ground for cultivating skills that will benefit you throughout life. Communication, time management, and teamwork are just a few of the competencies you'll develop, which are invaluable in both personal and professional contexts. Moreover, part-time jobs can often provide a glimpse into potential career paths, offering a practical understanding of what various professions entail, which can be instrumental in future education and career choices.

Workplace Rights and Safety

Understanding your rights as an employee is crucial. No matter how small the job may seem, knowing the laws that protect you— including regulations about minimum wage, work hours, and safety standards—is vital. For instance, many regions have specific labor laws designed to protect minors. These might dictate how many hours you can work during school weeks and what types of work you're permitted to do. Familiarize yourself with these regulations to ensure that your work environment is not just enriching but also safe and fair. Websites like the Department of Labor can provide resources and more detailed information specific to your locale.

Balancing Work and School

Managing both school responsibilities and a job can be a juggling act. It requires discipline and a well-thought-out plan to ensure one doesn't negatively impact the other. Prioritize your tasks, use a planner—digital or paper—to keep track of both school deadlines and work shifts and don't hesitate to communicate with your employer about your school commitments. Most employers are willing to accommodate your academic schedule, especially when they're informed in advance. Remember, while earning money is important, your education is invaluable and should remain a top priority.

Time Management Strategy: A Tool for Balancing Responsibilities

To further help you balance work and school, consider this simple yet effective time management strategy. Create a weekly schedule that includes all your fixed commitments, like school hours, study time, and work shifts. Then, identify blocks of free time that can be used for homework, relaxation, or attending to personal projects. By visually laying out your week, you can better manage your time and ensure that you're not overcommitting yourself, which is essential for maintaining a healthy balance between work, school, and personal life. This exercise helps you with your current schedule and develops a skill that will benefit you throughout your life.

As you embark on this exciting phase of earning your own money, remember that each job, no matter how small, holds valuable lessons and experiences. Whether it's the satisfaction of earning your first paycheck, the skills you develop, or the people you meet along the way, each experience contributes to your growing understanding of the world of work and finance. So, step confidently into this part of your maze, ready to explore, learn, and grow.

2.2 SIDE HUSTLES FOR TEENS: TURNING PASSIONS INTO PAYCHECKS

Turning what you love doing into a potential income source is like discovering you can turn sunlight into energy; it's not only exciting but empowering. Let's explore how you, as a teen, can transform your hobbies and skills into profitable side hustles. This isn't about taking on jobs that simply pay the bills but about creating opportunities that align with your passions and interests, giving you money, satisfaction, and a deep sense of achievement.

Identify Your Skills and Interests

First things first: take a moment to think about what you genuinely enjoy doing or what you're naturally good at. Perhaps you are good at explaining complex math problems, making your own jewelry, or editing videos until they look just right. These interests and skills are the perfect starting points for a side hustle. For example, tutoring younger students could be lucrative if you're great at a particular subject. If you're artistic, selling handmade crafts or artwork online might be your niche. And if tech is your thing, offering services like website design or video editing can attract clients even at a young age. Begin by listing all your skills and interests, no matter how trivial they might seem. Sometimes, even your quirkiest hobby can turn into a profitable venture.

Setting Up a Side Business

Once you've identified a potential side hustle, setting it up in a structured way can help turn sporadic opportunities into a steady income stream. Start with simple branding; choose a catchy name and create a basic logo using free online tools to make your business look professional right from the start. Understanding basic accounting is also crucial. Keep track of all money coming in and going out using a simple spreadsheet. This will help you see how your business is performing and make it easier to manage your earnings.

Marketing your services or products is the next big step. In today's digital world, a solid online presence can help attract customers from all over. Set up a professional profile on social media platforms relevant to your offerings. For instance, Instagram and Pinterest are great for visual-based services like photography or crafts, while LinkedIn could be more suitable for academic tutoring or tech services. Share your projects, customer testimonials, and special offers to engage with your audience and grow your customer base. Remember, every post is a reflection of your business, so keep it professional and true to your brand.

Utilizing Digital Platforms

The internet has opened up opportunities for selling products and services. Platforms like Etsy are perfect for selling handmade items, while Fiverr and Upwork are great for offering digital services such as graphic design, writing, or coding. These platforms provide a ready audience and handle many aspects of the business process, such as payments and marketing, allowing you to focus on perfecting your craft and fulfilling orders. However, it's important to understand the fees involved and how they might affect your pricing and profits.

Legal and Financial Considerations

As exciting as it is to earn your own money, it's essential to be aware of the legal and financial responsibilities that come with it. Depending on where you live, there may be regulations about how much a minor can work and earn without affecting their status as a dependent. If your side hustle turns into a significant income source, you might also need to pay taxes. Familiarize yourself with the basics of self-employment taxes in your area. A good rule of thumb is to set aside a portion of each payment for tax purposes, ensuring you're not caught off-guard when tax season rolls around. Additionally, if you're under 18, some aspects of your business, like setting up payment systems or signing contracts, might require parental consent or involvement.

Engaging in a side hustle as a teen supplements your income and builds invaluable skills that can benefit you throughout life. It teaches responsibility, enhances your understanding of business, and can even spark a lifelong passion for entrepreneurship. Whether it's through crafting, coding, or curating content, each step you take in developing your side business is a step towards growing your independence and achieving your financial goals.

2.3 UNDERSTANDING YOUR PAYCHECK: TAXES AND DEDUCTIONS EXPLAINED

When you receive your first paycheck, it might feel like a ticket to financial freedom. However, before you plan how to spend your hard-earned money, it's essential to understand what that slip of paper actually represents and why it looks the way it does. A paycheck isn't just a note from your employer saying, "Here's the money you earned." It's a detailed document showing what you've earned, what's been taken out, and why. Let's closely examine a typical paycheck to demystify its components.

Your paycheck has several key parts, starting with 'gross pay,' which is the total amount you've earned during the pay period before any deductions are made. Think of gross pay as the whole pie before anyone takes a slice. From this amount, various slices are taken out for different purposes, leading us to 'net pay'—what actually ends up in your pocket or bank account. This is your gross pay minus all the deductions, and it's usually a sobering moment to see how much of your pie has been shared.

The deductions from your gross pay typically include taxes, which are contributions to state and federal services, and may also include others like health insurance premiums or retirement savings if you've opted into those programs. The most common tax deductions you'll see are for federal income tax, state income tax (if applicable), Social Security, and Medicare. Understanding why these taxes are withheld brings us to an essential concept: tax withholding.

Tax withholding is the practice of deducting taxes from an employee's gross earnings to pay government taxes directly from your wages. The reason behind this is to spread your tax obligations over the entire year, which helps both the government manage its finances and you to avoid a large tax bill during tax season. Managing your withholdings effectively is crucial. If too much is withheld, you're giving the government a free loan until you file your taxes and potentially get a refund. If too little is withheld, you might face a hefty bill at tax time. You can adjust your withholdings by submitting a new W-4 form to your employer if you find that your situation isn't accurately reflected.

Moving on, contributions to Social Security and Medicare are also important to understand. These programs provide benefits for older adults, people with disabilities, and children if their working parents pass away. When you see 'FICA' on your paycheck, which stands for Federal Insurance Contributions Act, it refers to the taxes that fund Social Security and Medicare. You contribute a portion of your earnings to these programs, and your employer matches this contribution. Even though these benefits seem a long way off when you're a teenager, starting to contribute early helps ensure that these safety nets are funded and potentially available for you in the future.

Finally, let's talk about the documents you receive at the end of the year, particularly the W-2 form. This document summarizes your annual earnings and the total taxes withheld. It's crucial for filing your tax returns accurately. The W-2 form is mailed to you by your employer, usually by the end of January each year. It's important to keep this document in a safe place because you'll need it to prove your income when you file your taxes. It also serves as a check to ensure your employer has correctly reported your earnings and withholdings to the IRS.

Understanding each part of your paycheck is more than just a practical necessity. It empowers you to make informed decisions about your earnings and your financial future. Each line on your paycheck tells a story of where your money is going and provides insights into how you can manage it better. With this knowledge, you're better equipped to plan your spending, save wisely, and fulfill your obligations without stress. This transparency in where your money goes is not just enlightening; it's essential for taking control of your financial journey as you move from your first part-time job towards greater financial independence.

2.4 FINANCIAL RESPONSIBILITY: HANDLING YOUR MONEY WITH CARE

Stepping into the world of earning your own money, whether from a job or a side hustle, brings a surge of independence. It's exhilarating, right? Yet, with this new-found financial freedom comes the responsibility of managing that money wisely. Let's discuss how you can nurture your finances carefully, ensuring they grow and support you not just today, but well into the future.

Firstly, it's vital to get into the habit of regularly revisiting and adjusting your budget. Think of your budget as a living document that evolves as your financial landscape changes. Initiate this habit, especially after significant changes in your income or expenses, such as starting a new job or launching a side hustle. Reflect on how these changes impact your monthly cash flow. Maybe you have more income because you started tutoring, or your expenses have increased due to travel costs for a new part-time job. Adjust your budget accordingly to accommodate these changes, ensuring you always have a clear picture of your finances. This continuous process helps you stay aligned with your financial goals and prevents any surprises that could throw you off your path.

Moreover, the importance of saving cannot be overstated. It's tempting to spend all your hard-earned money on immediate wants, especially when you're young. However, saving a portion of every paycheck or income from side hustles is crucial. Start by setting clear, achievable goals. Maybe you want to build an emergency fund, which is essentially financial padding that helps you handle unexpected expenses without stress. Or perhaps you're saving for a major purchase or investment in your future, like college tuition or a first car. Whatever your goals, committing to saving regularly builds a solid financial foundation and instills discipline that benefits every area of your life.

Now, let's talk about avoiding common financial pitfalls. Overspending on non-essentials can quickly derail your financial stability. It's easy to fall into the trap of impulse buys or lifestyle inflation, where increased income leads to increased spending. Always question the necessity and value of each purchase. Additionally, steer clear of high-interest traps like payday loans or credit card debt, which can seem like quick fixes but often lead to deeper financial problems due to their crippling interest rates and fees. Developing good spending habits and learning to differentiate between wants and needs early on can save you from these common financial missteps.

Lastly, seeking financial advice is a smart move. No one expects you to navigate the complexities of financial management alone. There are numerous reputable sources you can turn to. Start with family members or someone you know who is good with money; they can provide personal insights and advice that's immediately applicable. School counselors are also a valuable resource, especially for college planning and scholarship opportunities. Additionally, there are numerous online resources and financial literacy websites that offer guidance tailored to young people. Just ensure you're consulting reliable sources, and when in doubt, double-check the information with other trusted advisors or platforms.

Navigating your financial responsibilities doesn't have to be daunting. By regularly adjusting your budget, committing to saving, avoiding common financial pitfalls, and seeking reputable advice, you're setting yourself up for a stable and prosperous financial future. Remember, the habits you form now will pave the way for your financial health as an adult.

As we wrap up this exploration of earning and managing your money, reflect on how these practices benefit your wallet and enrich your understanding and confidence in handling finances. You're building a toolkit that will support you throughout life, from your first paycheck to major financial decisions down the road. Next, we'll delve into making informed decisions about spending, ensuring that your money sustains you and enables you to enjoy life's pleasures without compromising your financial well-being.

CHAPTER THREE

SPENDING WISELY

Navigating the landscape of personal finance, especially when it comes to spending, can sometimes feel like being a goalkeeper in a high-stakes soccer game. Every decision to spend is a shot coming your way, and you must decide whether to block it or let it through. This chapter is about equipping you with the skills to make those decisions wisely, ensuring that your financial goals remain secure, and investing in your future with every dollar you spend. Let's dive into understanding the critical difference between needs and wants, how to allocate your budget effectively, and the art of delayed gratification.

3.1 NEEDS VS. WANTS: A GUIDE TO SMART SPENDING

Clarify the Difference

Understanding the difference between needs and wants is foundational in mastering smart spending. Needs are essentials necessary for basic living and functioning; they are the non-negotiables.

These include food, shelter, basic clothing, and a certain level of communication tools like a smartphone for school or work in today's connected world. Conversely, wants are items or services that enhance or improve your quality of life but are not essential for basic functioning. This category might include the latest smartphone model when you already have a functioning one, designer clothes, or dining out at upscale restaurants.

Let's consider a practical example to illustrate this further. Imagine you have a smartphone that works perfectly fine; it's fast enough for your needs, takes decent photos, and keeps you connected. However, a new model has just been released. It has better camera capabilities and a sleeker design. The new phone is a 'want,' not a 'need,' because your current phone serves all necessary functions. Recognizing this difference is crucial as it guides you in making spending decisions that align with your financial goals and not just your desires.

Budget Allocation

Once you have differentiated your needs from your wants, the next step is allocating your budget accordingly. Always prioritize your needs to ensure that your essential expenses are covered each month. This might mean setting aside a portion of your income or allowance immediately upon receiving it to cover things like transportation costs for school or essential phone bills. After your needs are budgeted for, you can consider how much of your remaining funds can be allocated to your wants.

One effective method for managing this is the 50/30/20 rule, which suggests spending 50% of your income on needs, 30% on wants, and saving the remaining 20%. This rule is not rigid; it's customizable based on your specific circumstances and financial goals. However, it serves as a helpful guideline in maintaining a balance between covering essential expenses, enjoying life's pleasures, and building your savings.

Delayed Gratification

Mastering the art of delayed gratification is a powerful tool in your financial toolkit. It involves resisting the immediate temptation of an unnecessary purchase and instead focusing on saving towards a more meaningful or high-quality item later on. The benefits of this approach are numerous. Not only does it help you avoid impulsive spending, but it also allows you to save for higher-quality items that may offer better longevity and satisfaction in the long run.

For instance, suppose you're considering buying a new laptop. You could buy a cheaper model now, which might serve your immediate needs but could become obsolete or start malfunctioning within a year or two. Alternatively, by practicing delayed gratification, you could save up for a few more months and invest in a higher-end model that would perform better and last longer. This approach ensures you get better value for your money and teaches you patience and strategic planning, invaluable in all areas of life.

Interactive Budgeting Exercise

To help you apply these concepts, let's engage in an interactive budgeting exercise. Imagine you have a monthly income or allowance of $500. Using the 50/30/20 rule:

- Calculate how much money you should ideally allocate to your needs, wants, and savings.
- List your typical monthly expenses under 'needs' and 'wants.'

- Adjust these figures to fit the 50/30/20 allocation, and identify any areas where you might need to cut back.

This exercise helps you visualize how to balance your spending and reinforces the discipline needed to maintain this balance. Regularly reviewing and adjusting your budget according to this framework ensures that your spending habits support your long-term financial well-being.

As we continue to explore the various facets of spending wisely, remember that each decision you make—whether it's distinguishing between a need and a want, allocating your budget, or practicing delayed gratification—is a step towards securing your financial future. Each wise spending choice is a building block in the foundation of your financial independence and stability.

3.2 EMOTIONAL SPENDING

Emotional spending is a familiar scene; you're feeling down, so you buy something to lift your spirits, or you're celebrating, so you treat yourself. It's normal to experience emotions that drive you to spend, but when not managed, these impulses can disrupt your financial stability and long-term goals. Understanding the emotional and environmental triggers that lead to such spending can empower you to keep your financial health in check.

Let's dive into the world of emotional triggers. Emotions powerfully influence our spending habits. Feelings of sadness, stress, or loneliness can make the idea of buying something new feel like a quick fix to improve our mood. On the other side, feelings of happiness and celebration can also lead to spending to amplify the good vibes. Retail therapy isn't just a phrase; it's a real phenomenon where shopping becomes a way to seek relief or momentary happiness. However, the relief is often temporary, and the financial consequences can be long-lasting. For example, consider a scenario where you had a tough week at school and decided to buy a new video game to feel better. It might help you unwind, but if these purchases become a regular habit whenever you're stressed, they can quickly eat into your savings or funds meant for other important needs.

Now, let's consider impulse buying, which often goes hand-in-hand with emotional spending. This type of spending is typically unplanned and can be triggered by various factors. Marketing tactics are particularly potent triggers. Stores are designed to entice you to buy more through sales signs, strategic product placements, and even through scents and lighting. Online stores use algorithms to suggest items that catch your eye based on your browsing patterns. Special offers like "buy one get one free" or "limited time offer" create a sense of urgency and can make it hard to resist making a purchase. Every time you give in to these tactics without considering if you truly need the item, you're making a dent in your financial plans.

One effective strategy for combating emotional and impulse spending is the 24-hour rule. When you feel the urge to buy something non-essential, give yourself 24 hours to think about it. This pause can diminish the impulse and give you time to consider whether you need the item or are just trying to fill an emotional void. Often, you'll find that the desire to buy fades after some reflection, and you'll feel relieved not having spent the money.

Another practical approach is to make a shopping list before you go to the store or log into an online shopping site. Stick to this list rigorously. It's a simple but powerful way to avoid buying things you don't need. Setting spending limits for different categories of your budget can also keep your finances on track. For instance, you might allocate a certain amount each month to personal treats or entertainment. Once that limit is reached, you know it's time to stop spending in that category. This helps keep your finances balanced and trains you to enjoy treats within a sustainable financial framework.

Navigating emotional spending is about recognizing the feelings that propel you to shop and implementing strategies to manage those impulses. By doing so, you maintain control over your financial decisions, ensuring that each purchase is thoughtful and truly adds value to your life. This mindful approach to spending protects your wallet and builds a foundation of financial discipline that will support your economic well-being for years to come.

3.3 ONLINE SHOPPING SMART: AVOIDING TRAPS AND SCAMS

Navigating the digital marketplace can sometimes feel like moving through a bustling city market, where every corner offers new delights and potential drawbacks. The convenience of purchasing everything from clothes to gadgets online can't be overstated, but it also comes with its own set of challenges, particularly the risk of scams and unsafe transactions. By adopting safe online shopping practices, you'll protect your money and enhance your shopping experience. Let's delve into how you can shop online securely, recognize scams, use comparison tools effectively, and understand the critical importance of return policies and guarantees.

Safe Online Practices

When shopping online, the foremost thing you should ensure is that your website is secure. This is easily identifiable by looking for 'HTTPS' rather than just 'HTTP' in the URL. The 'S' at the end stands for 'secure,' which means the data you enter is encrypted, protecting it from hackers. Another symbol of a secure site is a padlock icon next to the URL in the browser. Always avoid making purchases from sites that don't display these security indicators, as entering your payment information could expose you to the risk of fraud.

Using secure payment methods is another critical aspect of safe online shopping. Credit cards are generally safer than debit cards because they don't directly withdraw funds from your bank account and offer better fraud protection. Services like PayPal or Apple Pay also provide a secure layer as they obscure your financial details from the vendors, reducing the risk of your sensitive information being compromised. Moreover, avoiding saving your payment information on websites is a good practice. While storing your card details for future purchases is convenient, this convenience could cost you dearly if the site's security is breached.

Recognizing Scams

Phishing emails or messages that lure you into providing personal and financial information are common tactics used by scammers. These messages often mimic legitimate companies and may urgently ask you to update your payment information or confirm your password. Always be skeptical of unsolicited emails or messages that request sensitive information, even if they appear to be from a company you know. Verify the legitimacy of such communications by contacting the company directly using contact information from their official website. Do not use the contact details provided in the message.

Too-good-to-be-true deals are precisely that—unlikely to be true. Scammers often lure shoppers with the promise of high-value items at incredibly low prices. These deals may exist on spoofed websites that look remarkably similar to genuine online retailers. Always double-check the domain name for any subtle misspellings or odd characters that might indicate a fake site. Remember, if a deal seems too good to be true, it probably is, and it's best to steer clear.

Comparison Shopping

One of the best strategies to ensure you're getting a good deal while shopping online is to use comparison tools and apps. These tools allow you to compare prices across various online stores, helping you find the best deal for the product you want. Furthermore, reading customer reviews can provide insights into the quality of the product and the reliability of the seller. Reviews can be a valuable resource, revealing potential issues with the product or vendor that might not be evident from the description alone. However, be cautious of overly positive or repetitive reviews as they could be fabricated. Look for detailed reviews that discuss both pros and cons to get a balanced view.

Return Policies and Guarantees

Understanding the return policies and guarantees of products is essential when shopping online. Always read these policies carefully before making a purchase. They can vary significantly between different sellers and products. A good return policy should allow you sufficient time to receive and evaluate the product and return it if it doesn't meet your expectations or is defective. Be wary of vendors who do not provide clear return policies or charge hefty restocking fees. Knowing the return policy can save you from potential headaches if you need to return a purchase. Additionally, check for product guarantees and warranties that can provide further protection and peace of mind.

By embracing these smart online shopping practices, you equip yourself with the knowledge and tools to navigate the digital marketplace confidently and securely.

3.4 THE TRUE COST OF PEER PRESSURE: KEEPING UP VS. CATCHING UP

Navigating through your teen years, you'll find that one of the more subtle yet pervasive challenges is managing the influence of peer pressure, especially when it pertains to spending. It's not just about the direct nudges from friends to buy the latest gadgets or fashion items but also about the silent, scrolling pressure from social media, where every post can feel like a billboard advertising what you should own, wear, or experience to supposedly fit in. This kind of pressure doesn't just affect your social life; it deeply impacts your financial decisions and can have long-term effects on your financial health.

Let's consider the scenario of tech gadgets, which are often released in rapid succession. Each new smartphone or gaming console model comes with the allure of improved features and the promise of a better experience. The pressure to upgrade can be intense, especially when it seems like everyone in your circle or on your social media feed is flaunting the latest version. However, the financial reality of yielding to this pressure is significant. For instance, every year, upgrading to the newest smartphone model can cost thousands of dollars over time, money that could have been saved or invested for much larger returns. The key here is to evaluate the true value these upgrades bring to your life. Is the investment worth it, or is it merely a costly nod to staying within the trends?

The influence of peer pressure extends beyond just what you buy —it seeps into how you view your own value and decision-making prowess. Strengthening your self-confidence in making independent financial decisions is crucial. It's about understanding that true financial security comes from making choices that align with your personal and financial goals, not from adhering to the fleeting trends that crowd your social feeds. Building this kind of confidence starts with education and practice. The more you learn about managing money and making informed choices, the more empowered you become to resist the urge to spend just to keep up with others.

To resist peer pressure and foster genuine connections, consider engaging in social activities that aren't centered around spending. Activities like hiking, playing sports, or having game nights at home offer wonderful opportunities to enjoy time with friends without the added pressure of expensive outings. These activities allow relationships to flourish based on shared experiences rather than shared expenses. For instance, organizing a potluck movie night is budget-friendly and fosters a sense of community and belonging that no amount of money spent at a fancy restaurant can replicate.

Creating a shift in how you and your peers spend time together can also set a positive example, showing that fun and friendship are not commodities to be bought but experiences to be created and cherished. As you navigate through these social dynamics, remember that every choice you make—whether it's resisting an unnecessary upgrade or opting for a low-cost outing—strengthens your financial independence and sets a foundation for a future where you are in control of your finances, free from the costly influence of peer pressure.

3.5 BARGAIN HUNTING: TIPS FOR FINDING THE BEST IN DEALS

Thrifting through the maze of retail offers can sometimes feel like a treasure hunt. You're on a quest not just to find items that catch your eye, but to capture those that provide real value for your money. To transform you into a savvy bargain hunter, let's explore some effective tactics and resources that can help you snag the best deals without compromising on quality. From using coupons to mastering the art of negotiation, these strategies are designed to stretch your dollars further and make every purchase a victory in your personal finance journey.

Resources for Deals

The hunt for deals is exhilarating and, thanks to a variety of resources, it's also easier than ever. Coupons remain a goldmine for savings. You can find them in newspapers, direct mail pieces, or through dedicated coupon apps and websites that aggregate printable or digital coupons. Similarly, cashback apps and websites can put money back into your pocket after purchases. They work by giving you a percentage of your purchase back when you buy through their app or use a linked credit or debit card. Another rich hunting ground for bargains is the promotional offers during clearance sales and discount days like Black Friday or Cyber Monday. Many stores offer significant discounts these days, making them ideal for buying bigger-ticket items at a fraction of the cost. Keep an eye on your favorite stores and sign up for their newsletters to get early notifications about sales and exclusive offers.

Seasonal Shopping

Understanding the ebb and flow of retail pricing throughout the year can also lead to substantial savings. For instance, buying winter clothes at the end of the winter season or hitting back-to-school sales for tech products can be cost-effective strategies. Retailers often discount seasonal items to clear out inventory before the next season's stock arrives, which means that late winter (February and March) is a great time to scoop up winter apparel at a discount. Similarly, late August and early September can be optimal times to purchase laptops and tablets as stores cater to the back-to-school crowd with special offers.

Negotiation Skills

While not all shopping scenarios provide an opportunity to negotiate, places like flea markets, independent stores, and even yard sales can be ideal venues to practice bargaining. Start by doing your homework; know the value of the item you are interested in and the typical asking prices. Approach negotiation with a friendly attitude and a smile—being courteous can make the seller more willing to lower the price. Offer a reasonable counteroffer and be prepared to meet in the middle. Remember, the goal of negotiation is to reach a fair agreement where both you and the seller feel satisfied with the transaction.

Quality vs. Price

While finding the lowest price can be thrilling, balancing cost with quality is crucial. Opting for the cheapest option can sometimes lead to more expenses down the line if the item needs to be replaced sooner due to poor quality. Instead, aim for the best value —products that are priced affordably and built to last. Read reviews and check product ratings before making a purchase to ensure you are getting both quality and a great deal. This approach saves money in the long run and also aligns with environmentally friendly practices by reducing waste.

Navigating the world of deals and discounts is more than just about saving a few dollars—it's about making smart choices that benefit your financial state without sacrificing quality. By developing skills in using resources effectively, timing your purchases wisely, negotiating where possible, and constantly weighing quality against price, you equip yourself with the tools to make each purchase a considered decision. This strategy not only helps in managing your personal finances but also in building habits that contribute to a lifetime of wise spending.

As we close this chapter on spending wisely, remember that each strategy you employ—whether it's distinguishing between wants and needs, managing impulse spending, shopping safely online, handling peer pressure, or hunting for bargains—contributes to your broader financial goals. These practices are not just about saving money in the short term; they are about cultivating a financially savvy mindset that will serve you well throughout life.

Looking ahead, the next chapter will delve into the exciting world of saving and investing. We'll explore how you can grow your financial resources, not just preserve them. From the basics of setting up savings accounts to understanding the more complex landscape of investments, you'll learn how to transform your saved money into a growing asset that can support your dreams and goals in the years to come.

CHAPTER FOUR

SAVING AND INVESTING FOR THE FUTURE

Imagine for a moment that each dollar you save today is a seed you plant in the soil of your future. Just as a gardener nurtures their plants to see them bloom, your savings can grow and flourish, providing financial security and opening doors to future dreams and possibilities. This chapter is about empowering you with the knowledge to make your money work for you, transforming your savings from static figures in your bank account into dynamic assets that grow over time. Let's explore the compelling world of compound interest, a concept that might just change how you view saving altogether.

4.1 WHY START SAVING EARLY: THE MAGIC OF COMPOUND INTEREST

Explain Compound Interest

To understand compound interest, let's break it down with a simple analogy. Imagine you have a magical tree that drops one apple every day, and each of these apples can plant itself to grow a new apple tree. Initially, your growth seems slow; you have one apple, then two, and so on. However, as more trees grow, they too start dropping apples, exponentially increasing the number of apples you gather each day. Compound interest works similarly with your money.

Here's the math behind it: suppose you start with $100 in a savings account with an annual interest rate of 5%, compounded yearly. After the first year, you earn 5% of $100, which is $5, so you now have $105. In the second year, you earn 5% on $105, not just the original $100, which comes out to $5.25, bringing your total to $110.25. This process continues year after year, with the interest each year calculated on the new total. The magic here is that you're earning interest not just on your original amount, but also on the interest from previous years. Over time, this leads to increasingly larger growth, much like the apple trees in our analogy.

Real-Life Examples

To illustrate the power of starting early, consider two friends, Jamie and Alex, who decide to save for retirement. Jamie starts saving $200 a month at age 20, while Alex starts saving the same amount per month, but doesn't begin until age 30. Assuming they both earn a steady interest rate of 5%, compounded monthly, by the time they both retire at age 65, Jamie will have accumulated approximately $402,492, whereas Alex will have accumulated about $234,600. The ten-year head start gives Jamie's savings significantly more time to grow through the power of compound interest, illustrating why starting early can make such a big difference.

Interactive Compound Interest Calculator

To see the potential impact of compound interest on your own savings, I recommend exploring using an online compound interest calculator. These tools allow you to input different scenarios—changing the initial amount, the monthly contribution, the interest rate, and the number of years—to see how your money could grow over time. It's an eye-opening way to visualize the future potential of your current savings. Getting started can be a great motivator if you haven't already.

Motivate with Goals

Setting long-term financial goals can provide direction and purpose to your saving efforts. Whether saving for college, a car, or even early retirement, each goal can be significantly bolstered by the power of compound interest. Start by defining your goals clearly and then calculate how much you need to save regularly to achieve them. Making your goals specific, measurable, and tied to a clear timeline makes them more tangible and attainable. Remember, each step you take today in saving and understanding how your money can grow is a step toward securing a financially stable and fulfilling future.

As you begin applying compound interest principles to your savings strategy, think of yourself as the gardener we imagined earlier. Each dollar you save is a seed, and your knowledge of compound interest is the water and sunlight that helps it grow. By starting early, remaining consistent, and staying informed about how to optimize your savings, you're setting yourself up for a lush and vibrant financial future. Now, let's continue nurturing our financial garden by exploring more ways to make our money grow through smart saving strategies and initial forays into the world of investing.

4.2 INTRODUCTION TO INVESTING: STOCKS, BONDS, ETFS, AND MUTUAL FUNDS

As you begin to think about growing your savings, it's essential to understand various investment vehicles and how they can play a role in your financial strategy. Let's start with stocks, which are essentially small pieces of a company. When you buy a stock, you're buying a share of that company's earnings and assets. Stocks are known for their potential high returns, but they also come with risks, as their value can fluctuate quite a bit based on how well the company is doing and how the overall market is performing.

Bonds, on the other hand, are more like loans that you give to companies or governments in exchange for periodic interest payments plus the return of the bond's face value when it matures. The risk with bonds is generally lower than with stocks because you expect to get a certain amount of money back unless the issuer defaults. However, the returns on bonds are usually lower compared to stocks.

Then there are Exchange-Traded Funds (ETFs), which are groups of different stocks or bonds. An ETF tracks an index, a commodity, or a group of assets like an index fund but trades like a stock on an exchange. ETFs often offer lower expense ratios and fewer broker commissions than buying the stocks individually. They provide a good balance between the high potential returns of individual stocks and the lower risk of bonds.

Mutual funds are another option, similar to ETFs, but instead of being traded on an exchange, they are managed by financial professionals who try to outperform the market with the pool of money collected from many investors. Mutual funds offer diversification and professional management but often come with higher fees than ETFs, and their performance can vary widely depending on the managers' skills.

Start Small with Simulations

Before diving into real investments, it's a smart move to practice with simulations. Many online platforms offer virtual trading, where you can invest using fake money in real stock markets. This experience can be incredibly valuable. It allows you to understand market dynamics and test your investment strategies without any risk. You'll see how different factors affect your investments and how to react to market fluctuations, all in a controlled, stress-free environment.

Advice on Initial Investments

When you're ready to start investing for real, it's generally wise to start small. Many platforms now allow you to buy fractional shares of stocks or ETFs, which means you can invest in expensive stocks without having to buy a whole share. This can be a great way to get started with a smaller amount of money. Always remember, the key to successful investing is diversification—spreading your investments across various types of assets (stocks, bonds, ETFs) to reduce risk.

It's also crucial to choose the right platform. Look for apps or brokers that cater to young investors or those just starting out. They often offer educational tools, simple user interfaces, and low fees, which can make your initial foray into investing more manageable and less intimidating.

Understand Market Fluctuations

Investing can sometimes feel like a roller coaster. The markets go up and down, influenced by everything from economic data, corporate earnings, and interest rates to global events and market sentiment. However, it's important to keep a long-term perspective. Markets might fluctuate in the short term, but historically, they have trended upwards over the long term.

This is where the importance of patience comes in. Avoid making decisions based on short-term volatility; panic selling can lock in losses and miss out on potential gains when markets rebound. It's often those who stay the course, investing consistently over time, who see the best returns. Educate yourself about market cycles and learn to view dips as potential buying opportunities, not just risks.

By understanding these fundamental concepts and starting your investment journey thoughtfully, you're laying down a solid foundation for future financial growth. Remember, investing isn't just about making money quickly; it's about setting the stage for a lifetime of financial security and achieving your dreams. Whether those dreams are buying a home, traveling the world, or securing a comfortable retirement, becoming savvy about investing is a crucial step toward realizing them.

4.3 UNDERSTANDING RETURN ON INVESTMENT (ROI)

When you're ready to dip your toes into the world of investing, one term you'll frequently encounter is 'Return on Investment', commonly abbreviated as ROI. This metric is essential for assessing how effectively your money is working for you in any given investment. Think of ROI as a tool that helps you measure the success of your investment choices, much like how a report card reflects your academic performance. It tells you the percentage of money gained or lost on an investment relative to the amount of money invested.

To calculate ROI, you use a simple formula: (Net Profit / Cost of Investment) x 100. Let's break this down with an example. Suppose you invest $100 in a company's stock, and after a year, you sell your shares for $120. Your net profit from this investment is $20. Using the ROI formula, your calculation would be ($20 / $100) x 100, which equals a 20% ROI. This means you've made a 20% return on your initial investment, which is a clear and straightforward way to understand how beneficial or profitable your investment has been.

While calculating ROI is relatively simple, several factors can affect the outcome of this calculation, making the context as crucial as the numbers themselves. Market conditions play a significant role. For instance, a booming market can boost the ROI on your investments as increased demand for stocks generally pushes prices up. Conversely, in a recession, you might see a lower ROI or even a negative ROI if market prices fall and you sell your stocks for less than what you paid. Economic factors such as changes in interest rates, inflation, or employment rates can also influence investment returns. High interest rates, for instance, can reduce ROI by making borrowing more expensive, which might slow down economic growth and, subsequently, the growth of your investments.

Individual investment choices also significantly impact ROI. Different types of investments come with varying levels of risk and potential return. Stocks might offer high ROI potential but with considerable risk, whereas bonds generally provide lower ROI with less risk. Your ability to research and select investments that align with your financial goals and risk tolerance is crucial in maximizing ROI. For example, if you're saving for a short-term goal, you might choose a less risky investment, even if it means accepting a lower ROI, to ensure you don't lose your principal investment amount.

Using ROI effectively in making investment decisions involves more than just calculating percentages; it requires a comprehensive approach to evaluating opportunities. When considering an investment, look beyond the potential ROI and consider the investment's risk level, how it fits with your other investments (your investment portfolio balance), and how it aligns with your long-term financial goals. For instance, investing in a startup could offer a high potential ROI, but it also comes with high risk, which might not be suitable if you're planning to use your investment funds for a definite purpose in the near future, like funding your college education.

To practice and become more comfortable with these concepts, consider analyzing different investment scenarios using the ROI formula. You could create hypothetical investment situations or use past investment data to calculate ROI and discuss what factors might have influenced the results. This exercise helps consolidate your understanding of ROI and enhances your ability to apply this metric in real-world investing situations. Remember, the goal of using ROI isn't just to pick the investments with the highest returns but to choose the ones that best fit your overall financial strategy, balancing risk and reward in a way that helps you achieve your financial dreams and security.

4.4 USING DIGITAL TOOLS TO BOOST YOUR SAVINGS

In an era where technology intertwines with almost every aspect of our lives, harnessing the power of digital tools can significantly enhance your financial journey, especially when it comes to saving. As you navigate through the vast sea of apps and online resources, choosing the right ones can make a substantial difference in how effectively you manage and grow your savings. Let's explore several reputable financial apps that are designed to help you track savings, set and achieve budget goals, and visualize your financial growth, all of which are geared towards empowering you, the savvy teen saver.

Financial apps like Credit Karma, YNAB (You Need A Budget), and Acorns offer unique features tailored to enhance your savings strategy. Credit Karma, for example, provides a comprehensive overview of your finances by connecting all your accounts in one place, tracking your spending, and offering personalized insights on where you can cut costs and save more. YNAB focuses on proactive budget management, helping you allocate every dollar you earn towards specific spending categories or savings goals, ensuring you live within your means and save consistently. Acorns, on the other hand, introduces you to the world of investing by automatically investing your spare change from daily purchases into diversified portfolios, making the act of investing routine and seamless.

The magic of these tools lies in their ability to organize your finances and provide real-time, actionable insights that help you make informed decisions. By setting clear visual representations of your savings goals and showing your progress towards them, these apps can significantly enhance your motivation to save. They turn abstract figures into tangible goals, whether saving for a new laptop or stashing away funds for college, making saving more engaging and rewarding.

Automate Savings

Automating the process is one of the most effective strategies to ensure you save consistently. Setting up automatic transfers to your savings account immediately after you receive your income can profoundly impact your ability to save without thinking about it. This method plays a crucial role in building your savings effortlessly. It works because it takes the decision to save out of your hands after you set it up, effectively turning your good intentions into action. Apps like Digit analyze your spending habits and automatically transfer small amounts that you won't likely miss from your checking account to your savings account. This tool makes saving so seamless that you might not even notice the money being set aside, yet these small amounts accumulate significantly over time.

Enhance Financial Literacy

While apps that help you manage and save your money are invaluable, those that offer educational content are equally important. They empower you with knowledge, which is just as critical as the tools themselves. Apps such as Investopedia, Khan Academy, and Acorns provide lessons on basic economic principles, the importance of saving, how to budget effectively, and more advanced topics like investing. These resources are tailored to gradually increase your financial literacy, ensuring you practice good financial habits and understand the reasons behind them, which is crucial for lifelong financial competence.

Security Practices

As you integrate these digital tools into your financial routine, understanding and implementing robust cybersecurity measures is paramount to protect your sensitive information. Always use strong, unique passwords for each financial app and enable two-factor authentication where available to add an extra layer of security. Be cautious about the networks you use when accessing your financial accounts; avoid public Wi-Fi and consider using a VPN (Virtual Private Network) to encrypt your internet connection. Regularly update your apps and devices to protect against the latest security vulnerabilities and be vigilant about phishing attempts—always verify the authenticity of communications requesting your financial details.

Navigating the world of personal finance as a teen might seem daunting at first, but with the right tools and knowledge, it becomes an empowering journey. By leveraging these digital resources, you can transform the way you save, making it more consistent, efficient, and secure. Remember, each step you take now in building and managing your savings with the aid of these tools is paving the way for a financially sound future, filled with possibilities. As you continue to explore and utilize these digital aids, you'll find that managing your finances becomes simpler, more engaging, and impactful in achieving your dreams.

4.5 RETIREMENT ACCOUNTS FOR TEENS: IT'S NEVER TOO EARLY TO PLAN

Thinking about retirement might seem a bit out of place while you're still in high school or just beginning college. However, starting to plan for retirement early can be one of the most financially astute decisions you make. Let's explore the world of retirement accounts, specifically focusing on options like Roth IRAs that are particularly advantageous for young investors like you.

Retirement accounts are special types of savings accounts that offer tax benefits to incentivize saving for your later years. Among these, Roth IRAs (Individual Retirement Accounts) are incredibly beneficial for young investors due to their tax structure. Unlike traditional IRAs, where contributions are tax-deductible, but withdrawals during retirement are taxed, Roth IRAs work the opposite way. You contribute money that has already been taxed at your current, likely lower, tax rate. Then, the money grows tax-free, and you can withdraw it tax-free after you retire. This is particularly advantageous if you expect to be in a higher tax bracket in the future, as is often the case for young individuals starting their careers.

To illustrate the potential impact of starting a Roth IRA as a teen, consider this case study: Emily, a high school student, starts contributing $2,000 annually to her Roth IRA at age 16. Assuming an average annual return of 7%, by the time Emily reaches age 66, she would have contributed $100,000 over 50 years. However, thanks to the power of compound interest, her account balance would be approximately $1,068,048. In contrast, if she starts contributing the same amount annually but doesn't begin until age 26, her total contribution by age 66 would be $80,000, and her account balance would only grow to about $734,549. The additional ten years of compounding in the first scenario significantly boosts the growth of her retirement savings, showcasing the profound impact of starting early.

Opening a teen retirement account like a Roth IRA is a straightforward process, but there are a few key steps and eligibility requirements you should be aware of. Firstly, you must have earned income from a job to contribute to a Roth IRA, which means money from allowances or gifts doesn't count. The amount you can contribute is limited to what you've earned up to a maximum limit set by the IRS, which currently stands at $6,000 per year for individuals under 50. To open an account, you'll need to choose a provider—this could be a bank, a brokerage firm, or a robo-advisor. Each provider will have slightly different options and fees, so it's important to compare these to find the best fit for your needs. You'll typically need your Social Security number, proof of income, and a parent or guardian if you're under 18.

Once your account is set up, making regular contributions, even small ones, can lead to significant growth over time due to compound interest. For example, even contributing $50 a month, which might be a portion of what you earn from a part-time job, can grow substantially over the decades. Setting up automatic transfers from your checking account to your Roth IRA can make these contributions effortless, ensuring you consistently save without thinking about it each month.

By starting to save for retirement early, using accounts that grow tax-free, and making regular contributions, you're not just preparing for the distant future. You're also setting up financial habits that will benefit you throughout your life, ensuring you have the freedom and security to make choices that align with your aspirations. As you continue to explore and understand the various aspects of personal finance, remember that each step you take today is building towards a more secure and fulfilling tomorrow.

As this chapter closes, we reflect on the essential strategies and knowledge that empower you to grow your money and ensure long-term financial security. From understanding the basics of compound interest and the various types of investment vehicles to navigating the intricacies of retirement accounts, each topic we've covered contributes to a broader understanding of how to manage and grow your financial resources effectively. As you move forward, remember the importance of early planning, regular contributions, and informed decision-making in shaping a prosperous financial future.

In the next chapter, we'll shift our focus to protecting your hard-earned money, exploring topics such as insurance, identity protection, and avoiding common financial pitfalls. This knowledge is crucial, as safeguarding your assets is just as important as growing them.

CHAPTER FIVE

USING CREDIT WISELY

I magine you've just been handed the keys to a powerful sports car. It's sleek, fast, and packed with potential. But without the right knowledge and restraint, that power could lead to trouble. Credit, much like that sports car, is a powerful financial tool. When used wisely, it can enhance your financial flexibility and help build your future. However, when used recklessly, it can steer you toward financial mishaps. In this chapter, we'll navigate the ins and outs of credit cards—their benefits, risks, and how to use them responsibly. Let's buckle up and learn how to drive your financial journey with confidence and care.

5.1 THE ABCS OF CREDIT CARDS: WHAT EVERY TEEN NEEDS TO KNOW

Credit Card Basics

A credit card allows you to borrow money up to a certain limit to purchase items or withdraw cash, which you then pay back at a later date. This convenience, however, comes with responsibilities. Understanding the fundamental aspects such as interest rates, annual fees, credit limits, and minimum payments is crucial.

- Interest Rates: This is the cost of borrowing money from the credit card company. It's usually represented as an Annual Percentage Rate (APR). For instance, if you have an APR of 18% and you carry a balance of $100 on your credit card for a year, you'll pay around $18 in interest. However, if you pay off your balance in full each month, you generally won't have to pay any interest.
- Annual Fees: Some credit cards charge an annual fee for their use, ranging from $25 to several hundred dollars, depending on the card's benefits. Always weigh whether the benefits of the card outweigh the cost of the fee.
- Credit Limits: This is the maximum amount you can charge on your credit card. It can range from a few hundred to thousands of dollars and is determined by the credit card issuer based on factors like your income and credit history.
- Minimum Payments: This is the smallest amount you can pay on your balance each month to avoid fees and penalties. It's usually a percentage of your total current balance. Paying only the minimum can lead to more interest charges, significantly increasing the cost of the purchases.

Choosing Your First Credit Card

When selecting your first credit card, consider starting with a secured credit card. These require a cash deposit that typically serves as your credit limit. This deposit is security for the issuer and makes securing a card easier, even without a credit history. It's a valuable stepping stone to building credit responsibly.

When comparing cards, look at the interest rates and fees, but also consider other features like rewards programs or cash back on purchases. These can be beneficial, but they should never be the sole reason to spend. Always prioritize cards with lower interest rates and fees, especially when you're starting out.

Responsible Usage

Using a credit card wisely means recognizing it as a tool for convenience and credit building, not as an extension of your income. Aim to use your card for planned purchases only and avoid impulse buys. Always try to pay your balance in full each month to avoid interest charges, which can quickly accumulate and lead to debt.

Understanding the Statement

Each month, you'll receive a credit card statement either by mail or electronically. This document provides a detailed record of all transactions made with the card, fees charged, and payments made. It's essential to review your statement thoroughly to ensure all charges are accurate and to understand your spending patterns. Look out for unfamiliar charges and report them immediately, as they could be signs of fraud.

Visual Element: Interactive Element

Credit Card Statement Example: To visualize your understanding of reading a credit card statement, check out this link that shows you an example of a credit card statement from Ramsey Solutions (What You Need to Know About Reading Your Credit Statement - Ramsey (ramseysolutions.com)). You'll be presented with a sample statement and a series of questions to identify key components like the statement balance, minimum payment due, and any fees charged. This exercise will help you become proficient in monitoring your credit card activity and managing your account effectively.

Navigating the complexities of credit cards doesn't have to be intimidating. With the proper knowledge and a responsible approach, you can use them to your advantage, building a solid credit foundation that will benefit you long into the future. As you continue to learn and grow in your financial journey, remember that, like any powerful tool, the key to success is in how you use it. Use your credit wisely, and you'll be well on your way to a secure and prosperous financial future.

5.2 BUILDING AND MAINTAINING A HEALTHY CREDIT SCORE

Navigating the world of credit can often feel like learning a new language. Among the most crucial terms you'll encounter is the "credit score." This is a numerical expression based on a level analysis of your credit files, representing your creditworthiness, or in simpler terms, how reliable you are when it comes to paying back money you owe. Credit scores are calculated using information from your credit reports, including your payment history, the amounts you owe, the length of your credit history, new credit, and types of credit used. A higher score boosts your ability to obtain loans and credit cards and often secures lower interest rates and better terms. This can be particularly important when you're aiming to rent an apartment, secure a loan for a car, or even finance your first home.

Building a solid credit score early can set a positive tone for your financial dealings. One effective strategy is becoming an authorized user on a parent's credit card. This arrangement allows you to benefit from the primary holder's credit history without the obligation to make payments. It's like getting a head start in a race; you'll begin building your credit history as transactions are made, provided the primary account holder maintains a good payment record. Another foundational step is obtaining a secured credit card. With this type of card, you make a deposit that usually serves as your credit limit. It's a responsible way to build credit because it limits the risk of spending more than you can afford to pay back.

Regularly paying your bills on time cannot be overstated in its importance. Each timely payment positively impacts your credit score, demonstrating your reliability as a borrower. Conversely, late payments can significantly harm your score. Setting up automatic payments for recurring bills or setting reminders for due dates can help you maintain a consistent payment schedule, ensuring that your credit remains in good standing.

Monitoring your credit reports is another key aspect of maintaining a healthy credit score. You are entitled to a free credit report from each of the three major credit reporting agencies— Equifax, Experian, and TransUnion—once every twelve months, which you can obtain through AnnualCreditReport.com. Regularly reviewing your credit report allows you to verify that all the information is accurate and up to date. It also helps you spot any discrepancies or signs of identity theft early on. If you do find errors, you can dispute them with the credit bureau. This process involves sending a formal letter explaining the error, accompanied by any supporting documents. The bureau is then required to investigate and resolve your dispute, typically within 30 days. Keeping your credit report accurate is vital, as any errors can negatively impact your credit score and your future financial opportunities.

The benefits of maintaining a good credit score extend beyond just ease of borrowing. They include lower interest rates on loans and credit cards, which can save you thousands of dollars over time. A high credit score can also give you a better chance of approval for rental houses and apartments, as landlords often check credit scores to evaluate a tenant's reliability. Additionally, some employers check credit scores during the hiring process to assess a candidate's responsibility and integrity. Therefore, a good credit score supports your financial health and influences your housing situation and career opportunities.

As you move forward, remember that building and maintaining a healthy credit score is an ongoing process. It requires attention, consistency, and financial discipline, but the rewards are worth the effort. By taking deliberate steps to establish and preserve your creditworthiness, you are investing in your financial future, ensuring that when you need to rely on your credit, it's ready and robust enough to support your goals.

5.3 THE DANGERS OF DEBT: HOW TO USE CREDIT SAFELY

Navigating through the financial landscape, especially as a teen, can sometimes feel like you're walking a tightrope. One side represents the freedom and opportunities that credit offers, while the other side drops into the potential pitfalls of debt. It's crucial to understand the different types of debt and their impacts on your financial health. To put it simply, debt is the money you owe and must pay back, often with interest. The most common types include credit card debt, student loans, and personal loans.

Credit card debt is perhaps the most accessible form of debt for many teens, particularly once you start building your credit. It's also one of the easiest to accumulate due to the convenience and seeming invisibility of swiping a card. Student loans, on the other hand, are a significant source of debt for many young adults, but they're often considered an investment in your future earning potential. Personal loans, which can cover everything from car purchases to medical bills, typically come with higher interest rates and are used when immediate cash is needed.

In financial circles, you'll often hear terms like "good debt" and "bad debt." These aren't just labels; they represent how certain types of debt can either be an investment in your future or a financial burden. Good debt usually includes things like student loans or mortgages that increase your net worth or generate long-term income. Bad debt, such as high-interest credit card debt, doesn't increase your wealth and often includes purchases that depreciate quickly.

The impact of high interest rates on your financial stability cannot be overstated. Credit cards, for instance, can carry higher interest rates than most other forms of debt. If not managed properly, what started as a small debt can spiral into an overwhelming burden. For example, if you carry a $1,000 balance on a credit card with an 18% interest rate and only make the minimum payments, it could take years to pay off that debt, and you'd end up paying hundreds of dollars extra in interest. This kind of high-interest debt can quickly become a barrier to achieving your financial goals, like saving for college or buying a car.

When it comes to managing debt, having a clear strategy is critical. Techniques like the debt snowball or avalanche methods can be highly effective. The snowball method involves paying off your debts from smallest to largest, regardless of interest rate. This can be psychologically satisfying because you see debts disappearing quicker. The avalanche method, however, prioritizes debts with the highest interest rates, which can save you money on interest payments over time. Both methods require discipline and a solid understanding of your total debt picture.

Avoiding debt traps is another crucial skill. Payday loans and cash advances, for example, might seem like quick fixes when you're in a financial pinch, but they often exacerbate financial problems due to their sky-high interest rates and fees. If you are short on cash, consider safer alternatives like negotiating payment plans with creditors, seeking financial assistance from family, or consulting with a financial advisor. Always read the fine print and understand the full cost of borrowing money, whether it's from a bank, a payday lender, or through a credit card advance.

Understanding these aspects of debt and applying smart management strategies can protect you from the potential downsides of borrowing. Remember, while debt can be a useful financial tool when used wisely, it requires careful handling to ensure it doesn't hinder your financial future. As you continue to build your knowledge and experience with credit, keep these principles in mind to maintain a healthy balance between leveraging opportunities and avoiding financial pitfalls.

5.4 STUDENT LOANS: WHAT YOU SHOULD KNOW BEFORE BORROWING

Navigating the world of student loans can feel like preparing for a significant expedition. You're about to invest in your future, and the choices you make now will influence your financial landscape long after graduation. Understanding the types of student loans available, how much to borrow, and the terms of repayment are crucial steps in making informed decisions that align with your long-term financial health.

Student loans come in two primary types: federal and private. Federal student loans often include lower interest rates and more flexible repayment options compared to their private counterparts. They do not generally require a credit check, and the interest rates are fixed, which means they won't change over the life of the loan. This stability can be a significant advantage as it provides predictability in your financial planning. On the other hand, private student loans are typically offered by banks, credit unions, or other financial institutions. While they can cover additional expenses that federal loans might not, they usually come with higher interest rates that can be either fixed or variable and less flexible repayment terms. Plus, they often require a credit check, and having a co-signer is not uncommon.

When considering how much to borrow, it's crucial to adopt a mindset of restraint. While it can be tempting to take out the maximum amount offered, remember that every dollar borrowed is a dollar that must be paid back—with interest. Focus on borrowing only what you need to cover your educational expenses. To do this effectively, create a detailed budget considering tuition, books, supplies, housing, and other necessary expenses. Evaluate other resources like scholarships, grants, and part-time work, which could reduce the amount you need to borrow. This proactive approach helps minimize your debt load, making your financial management more manageable post-graduation.

Understanding the terms of repayment is another critical aspect of handling student loans effectively. Federal loans offer several repayment plans, including standard, graduated, and income-driven repayment plans. Each of these has its nuances. For example, income-driven repayment plans adjust your monthly payments based on your income and family size, which can be particularly beneficial if you start with a lower salary. Additionally, some federal loans offer forgiveness programs for those who work in public service or teaching. It's important to review each plan's details and consider how your expected future earnings align with the repayment schedule. This alignment ensures that you're not just making decisions based on your current financial situation but are also considering your financial growth and potential challenges.

Strategizing for repayment should begin even before you graduate. Consider setting aside any earnings from part-time jobs to start paying off the interest on your loans while still in school. This can significantly reduce the amount you'll owe later. Once you graduate, if you find yourself in a situation where the standard repayment plan is not feasible, consider options like loan consolidation or refinancing. These can often lower your interest rates or extend your repayment period to make monthly payments more manageable. However, they might also mean paying more in interest over the life of the loan, so it's important to crunch the numbers carefully and consider your long-term financial goals.

Navigating student loans responsibly sets the stage not just for your academic journey, but for a financially stable future. By understanding the types of loans available, borrowing only what you need, comprehending the repayment terms, and planning early for repayment, you're building a robust financial foundation that supports your educational aspirations and long-term economic well-being.

As we wrap up our discussion on student loans, remember that the decisions you make about borrowing can have lasting impacts on your financial health. The insights shared here aim to equip you with the knowledge to manage your student loans effectively, ensuring they are a tool for advancement rather than a burden. Next, we will explore protecting your financial interests, focusing on strategies to safeguard your assets and navigate potential financial challenges effectively. This next chapter is about fortifying the financial wisdom you've gained, helping you move forward with confidence and security.

# CHAPTER SIX

ADVANCED MONEY MANAGEMENT TECHNIQUES

I magine standing at the edge of a diving board, the water below clear and inviting. You know that once you jump, the way you've planned and prepared will determine the grace and impact of your dive. Managing your money as you grow older can feel like preparing for that jump—especially when saving up for something big. This chapter isn't just about saving up; it's about strategically planning and executing your financial decisions to ensure you make a splash in the most rewarding way possible.

6.1 ADVANCED BUDGETING: PLANNING FOR BIG PURCHASES

Setting Financial Targets

When you dream about buying your first car, backpacking across Europe, or even funding your college education, these aren't just fleeting wishes. They are significant financial goals that require careful planning and commitment. Setting financial targets begins with defining what you want to achieve and by when. For instance, if you're aiming to purchase a car when you turn eighteen, start by researching the costs associated with buying and maintaining a vehicle. This gives you a clear target to aim for.

Once you have a figure in mind, break it down into manageable parts. If that car will cost $10,000 and you have two years until you turn eighteen, you need to save about $417 per month. Setting such precise targets does more than just outline what you need to save; it provides a roadmap and sets a pace for your savings. It's also crucial to adjust these targets as your circumstances change. Maybe you get a part-time job that pays more than expected, or car prices increase. Regularly revisiting and adjusting your financial targets ensures they remain realistic and achievable.

Prioritizing Expenses

With your financial target set, the next step is aligning your current spending to support this goal. This means prioritizing expenses and ensuring your essential needs are met while finding areas where you can cut back to funnel more into your savings. Start by categorizing your spending into 'needs' (essentials like food, housing, and transportation) and 'wants' (non-essentials like eating out, entertainment, and luxury items).

You might need to adjust these categories to save for your big purchase. Perhaps you limit eating out from three times a week to once a week, or you opt for more budget-friendly entertainment options. Each decision to cut back on a 'want' is a step closer to your 'need,' which, in this case, is your big purchase. It's about making daily conscious choices that align with your financial goals, ensuring every dollar spent is a step in the right direction.

Tools for Budget Tracking

Utilizing advanced budgeting tools and software can be incredibly helpful in keeping your savings on track. These tools allow you to set up specific savings goals and track your progress toward them. They can provide visual representations of where your money is going, how your savings are growing, and how adjustments to your spending habits directly affect your goals. Apps like Credit Karma or You Need a Budget (YNAB) offer features where you can tag certain expenses and monitor how much you're allocating towards different goals. This keeps you motivated and provides tangible evidence of your financial discipline and progress.

Case Studies

Consider the story of Maria, a high school student who dreamed of taking a gap year to travel through Asia. By setting a target of $8,000, she planned her savings right from her sophomore year. Maria used budget-tracking apps to monitor her expenses, cutting back on monthly subscriptions and part-time job earnings. By her senior year, not only had she saved $8,500, but she also learned invaluable lessons about money management that prepared her for financial independence in college.

Then there's Alex, who wanted a new laptop for college. By prioritizing his expenses and saving diligently, he purchased them without dipping into his college fund while maintaining his essential expenses. These stories aren't just about achieving goals; they're about the empowerment and confidence that come from taking control of your finances.

Navigating through advanced budgeting techniques equips you with the skills to make informed and impactful financial decisions. Whether it's saving for a first car, a dream vacation, or college, the principles of setting clear targets, prioritizing expenses, using the right tools, and learning from real-life examples pave the way for financial success. As you move forward, remember that each step in this financial planning process is building your confidence and capability to manage bigger financial challenges that lie ahead.

6.2 FINANCIAL FORECASTING: PREDICTING YOUR MONEY'S FUTURE

Navigating your financial future can sometimes feel like reading a map in the dark. Financial forecasting is like turning on the light, giving you a more straightforward path to follow by predicting where your financial decisions today will lead you tomorrow. Essentially, it involves using your current financial data to make educated guesses about your future financial state. This process is critical in personal financial planning because it helps you anticipate and prepare for future needs, avoid pitfalls, and capitalize on opportunities.

Let's break down some basic forecasting methods like trend analysis and scenario planning. Trend analysis involves looking at your past financial data to identify patterns or trends that might continue into the future. For example, suppose you've consistently spent 30% of your income on dining out over the past year. In that case, you might forecast similar spending in the coming year unless you change this habit. Scenario planning, on the other hand, involves imagining different possible futures and planning for them. What would happen if you suddenly lost your part-time job or if car maintenance costs doubled? How would these scenarios impact your savings goals or your ability to pay for school? You can create more flexible and robust financial plans by considering different possibilities.

Now, how about putting these forecasting methods into practice using tools like spreadsheets? Spreadsheets can be incredibly powerful in financial forecasting. They allow you to organize your financial data, apply formulas to project future trends, and see the results of different scenarios with just a few keystrokes. Start by creating a basic spreadsheet where you track your monthly income and expenses. Then, use formulas to project these figures into the future based on your expected growth rates or changes. For instance, if you plan to start a side hustle, how will the additional income affect your savings rate? Or if you anticipate college expenses, how will this impact your monthly budget?

Exploring how different financial decisions impact your forecasts is the next vital step. Think about what happens if you adjust various elements like your savings rate, investment contributions, or discretionary spending. For example, increasing your savings rate by just a few percentage points could significantly accelerate your progress toward financial goals like buying a car or funding a gap year. Conversely, higher spending on non-essentials could delay these goals. Using your spreadsheet, model different scenarios like these to see how small adjustments can have big impacts over time. This exercise helps you understand the implications of your choices and empowers you to make informed decisions.

Lastly, the importance of regularly reviewing and adjusting your forecasts cannot be overstated. Your financial situation and goals will evolve over time, and so should your forecasts. Maybe you get a higher-paying job, receive an unexpected windfall, or face unforeseen expenses—any of these could significantly alter your financial trajectory. Make it a habit to revisit your financial forecasts at least once every quarter. Check if your actual finances are aligning with your projections and adjust your forecasts and budget accordingly. This regular review ensures that your financial plans always reflect your current reality and goals, allowing you to steer confidently toward your desired financial future.

As you continue to navigate through your financial landscape, remember that forecasting is not about predicting the future with certainty but about preparing for it with clarity and confidence. Using these forecasting tools and methods, you can illuminate the path ahead, making navigating life's financial challenges and opportunities easier.

6.3 WEALTH BUILDING STRATEGIES FOR TEENS

Understanding how to build wealth isn't just about accumulating money; it's about growing a sustainable financial ecosystem that supports your long-term prosperity. When you think about wealth, it's helpful to visualize a thriving garden. Just as a garden needs a variety of plants to flourish, your financial portfolio requires a mix of assets and investments. Assets aren't just piles of cash; they're resources that have the potential to increase in value over time, such as stocks, bonds, and real estate. By investing in these assets, you're essentially planting seeds that could grow into strong, resilient sources of wealth.

Investment diversification is a key strategy in wealth building. Just as a garden with only one type of plant can suffer from pests or bad weather, a portfolio with only one kind of investment can suffer from market volatility. Diversification means spreading your investments across different asset classes. This can help manage risk and reduce the impact of poor performance in any single investment. For instance, while stocks might offer high returns, they can be volatile. Bonds, on the other hand, generally provide steadier, though often lower, returns. Including real estate or commodities like gold can provide further balance, as these assets often behave differently from stocks and bonds. The idea is to create a portfolio that can withstand different economic climates, ensuring your financial growth is steady and sustainable.

Looking beyond the immediate, developing a long-term financial plan is crucial. This plan isn't just about saving for a distant retirement; it's about setting stages for financial growth throughout your life. Start by envisioning where you want to be in ten, twenty, or even thirty years. Do you see yourself owning a home, starting a business, or traveling the world? Each of these goals requires strategic financial planning and investments that align with your time frame and risk tolerance. Retirement planning, for instance, might focus on more conservative investments as you approach retirement age to preserve the wealth you've accumulated. On the other hand, if you're aiming to start a business in five years, your strategy might involve more aggressive investments to grow your capital more quickly. Regularly revisiting and adjusting this plan as your financial situation and goals evolve is essential. Life can change unexpectedly, and your financial plan should be flexible enough to accommodate those changes.

Ethical wealth building is another significant aspect to consider. As you grow your wealth, think about how your investments impact the world. Socially responsible investing (SRI) has gained traction, allowing investors to put their money into companies and funds that align with their ethical beliefs. This might mean investing in companies that prioritize environmental sustainability, social justice, or corporate ethics. By choosing investments that reflect your values, you're not just building wealth; you're supporting a financial structure that contributes positively to society. This approach can offer a profound sense of satisfaction, knowing that your financial success also promotes the well-being of others and the planet.

Navigating the complexities of wealth building as a teen might seem daunting, but it's a journey worth embarking on. By understanding the importance of assets, embracing diversification, planning strategically for the long term, and making ethical investment choices, you're laying down a strong foundation for financial success. This foundation supports your personal and financial growth. It aligns your financial practices with your values, creating a holistic approach to wealth that can guide you through various stages of life. As you continue to explore and apply these strategies, remember that each step you take builds your wealth and understanding of managing and preserving it effectively.

6.4 MANAGING MONEY ACROSS DIFFERENT PLATFORMS

Navigating the digital age means more than just being tech-savvy; it's about leveraging technology to enhance and simplify your financial life. Think of the countless digital financial platforms available today—from online banking and investment apps to peer-to-peer payment services—as tools in your financial toolkit. Each tool serves a unique purpose, whether it's helping you save, spend, invest, or even lend money more efficiently.

In online banking, for instance, you can manage your bank accounts from your smartphone or computer. This convenience allows you to check balances, transfer funds, pay bills, and deposit checks electronically without ever needing to visit a bank branch. Investment apps take this a step further by allowing you to track your investments and trade stocks, buy bonds, or experiment with newer asset classes like cryptocurrencies, all from your device. Then there are peer-to-peer payment services like Venmo, PayPal, or Cash App, which revolutionize how you send money, split bills, or receive payments, making transactions as simple as sending a text message.

However, with great convenience comes great responsibility, especially when it involves integrating these platforms into a cohesive financial management strategy. One effective approach is to use financial management apps that consolidate information from various accounts and platforms. These apps provide a comprehensive dashboard that gives you an overview of your financial status at a glance—your bank account balances, investment values, upcoming bills, and recent transactions all in one place. This integration not only helps in keeping track of your finances but also aids in making informed financial decisions based on a holistic view of your resources.

Security is paramount when managing finances online. Cyber threats are a real and present danger, making it crucial to adopt stringent cybersecurity practices. Begin with the basics: ensure all your financial accounts have strong, unique passwords. Consider using a password manager to keep track of them securely. Enabling two-factor authentication adds another layer of security, requiring not just a password and username but also something that only you, the user, have on them, like a fingerprint or a mobile device. Regular monitoring of your financial accounts for any unauthorized activity is also essential. Set up alerts that notify you of any unusual transactions, helping you act swiftly should there be any breach.

Periodically reviewing and consolidating your financial platforms can streamline your finances and save you money. Over time, it's common to accumulate accounts and subscriptions that you may no longer use. By reviewing your financial tools and accounts regularly, you can identify which services are redundant or under-used. Consolidating these can reduce clutter in your financial management practices and minimize fees or charges that may unnecessarily drain your resources. For instance, if you have multiple investment accounts with different brokers, consider whether it makes sense to consolidate them into one account to reduce fees and simplify your investment management strategy.

Managing your money across different platforms isn't just about using digital tools but optimizing them to create a more integrated, secure, and efficient financial management system. By embracing these technologies and practices, you're not just keeping up with the digital age; you're actively using it to forge a path toward a more secure and prosperous financial future.

This chapter explored the sophisticated strategies that can help you manage your finances across various digital platforms effectively. From integrating diverse financial tools to ensuring robust security measures, these strategies are designed not just for convenience but for enhancing your financial wellness. As we transition from understanding these digital tools to exploring deeper into protecting your financial interests in the next chapter, remember that each step you take builds upon your ability to navigate the complex world of personal finance with confidence and foresight.

Your gift costs no money and less than 60 seconds to make real, but can change a fellow teen's life forever. Your review could help…

- one more teen learn how to save money.
- one more teen understand the difference between needs and wants.
- one more teen start their first budget.
- one more teen make smart financial decisions.
- one more teen's dream come true.

To get that 'feel good' feeling and help this person for real, all you have to do is...and it takes less than 60 seconds...

leave a review.

Simply scan the QR code to leave your review:

If you feel good about helping a faceless teen, you are my kind of person. Welcome to the club. You're one of us.

I'm that much more excited to help you achieve financial independence easier than you can possibly imagine. You'll love the strategies I'm about to share in the coming chapters.

Thank you from the bottom of my heart. Now, back to our regularly scheduled programming.

Your biggest fan,
A. P. McMillan

PS - Fun fact: If you provide something of value to another person, it makes you more valuable to them. If you'd like goodwill straight from another teen - and you believe this book will help them - send this book their way.

CHAPTER SEVEN

FINANCIAL PLANNING FOR SIGNIFICANT EXPENSES

Picture this: you've just landed on the moon, and now you have to figure out how to live there. That's a bit of what planning for significant expenses like college can feel like—exciting, yes, but also a little daunting, especially when you're looking at the costs involved. But just as astronauts train extensively for their missions, you too can prepare for these financial challenges. This chapter is your training ground for one of the biggest expenses you might face soon—college. We'll walk through understanding the costs, exploring funding options, crafting a savings plan, and working with you to make your college dreams a reality.

7.1 SAVING FOR COLLEGE: A STEP-BY-STEP GUIDE

Assessing the Costs

Going to college isn't just about tuition. It's like an iceberg where tuition is what you see above the water, and below the surface, there are all sorts of other expenses—room and board, books, supplies, personal expenses, and possibly travel costs if you're going far from home. Breaking down these costs gives you a clearer picture of what you'll need to finance. Tuition can vary wildly depending on whether you choose a public or private college, in-state or out-of-state. Room and board can also differ based on the location; living in a big city usually costs more. Books and supplies can add up too, though there are ways to reduce these costs, like buying used textbooks or renting them. By outlining each of these expenses, you can start to see the whole financial landscape of college rather than just the tuition mountain peak.

Exploring Financial Aid Options

Now, let's talk about how you can gather the resources to tackle this financial challenge. There's a whole toolbox of financial aid options available to help manage college costs. Scholarships are like the golden tickets of college funding—they don't need to be repaid. Many are based on academic merit, but others are based on talents, interests, or other criteria. Grants are similar but are often need-based. Then there are work-study programs, which allow you to work part-time while studying, earning money to help cover your expenses. Finally, student loans need to be repaid, often with interest. Navigating these options might seem complicated, but resources like the FAFSA (Free Application for Federal Student Aid) can guide you through the process, helping you understand what financial aid you might be eligible for.

Creating a Saving Plan

You can start to build your savings plan with a clear understanding of the costs and aid options. Starting early is key. Consider high-yield savings accounts, which offer higher interest rates than regular savings accounts, allowing your money to grow faster. Another option is a 529 plan, a tax-advantaged savings plan designed specifically for education costs. These plans can vary from state to state but offer valuable tax benefits. You can build up your college fund over time by putting a portion of money aside regularly—whether from part-time jobs, allowances, or gifts. Even small amounts can add up, especially if you start early and make saving a consistent habit.

Family Financial Planning

Tackling college expenses is often a team effort. It's important to have open conversations with your family and adults in your life about expectations and contributions. Discuss who will be responsible for different expenses and how much you can realistically afford. These discussions can sometimes be difficult, but they are crucial in setting realistic goals and making sure everyone is on the same page. Planning together not only helps distribute the financial burden, but also ensures that everyone is committed to the common goal of their education.

Interactive Budget Worksheet

Let's work through an interactive budget worksheet to bring all this planning into a clear, actionable form. You can see a pdf visual example and use the interactive Excel template found on the Junior Achievement Teen Budgeting Income and Spending Worksheet found at this link (https://jausa.ja.org/programs/supple ments/ja-teen-budgeting-income-and-spending-worksheets).
This tool will help you list all potential sources of income and match them against the expenses we discussed. You'll be able to see how your savings, potential financial aid, and family contributions come together to meet your educational costs. Adjust

different variables to see how changes in your savings rate or additional scholarships can affect your overall budget. This exercise not only aids in visualizing your financial plan but also empowers you with the knowledge to adjust your strategy as circumstances change.

Navigating the financial aspects of college planning is no small feat, but with the right tools and a clear understanding of the costs and resources available, you can set yourself up for success. Remember, like any major journey, the key to success is preparation. By taking the time to assess all your options and start saving early, you're building a strong foundation to support your educational goals and financial well-being in the years to come.

7.2 BUYING YOUR FIRST CAR: FINANCIAL TIPS AND TRICKS

Imagine the freedom of driving your own car. Whether it's to school, work, or on weekend adventures, owning a car is a significant step towards independence. But before you get behind the wheel, it's crucial to understand the total cost of car ownership. It's more than just the price tag on the windshield; it includes ongoing expenses like insurance, maintenance, and fuel, not to mention the inevitable depreciation over time.

Let's break it down. The purchase price is what you pay to buy the car, either from a dealership or a previous owner. However, the costs don't stop there. Auto insurance is mandatory and can vary greatly depending on factors like your age, driving history, and the type of car you choose. Then there's maintenance—regular oil changes, tire rotations, and the occasional repair to keep your car running smoothly. Fuel is another ongoing cost, influenced by how much you drive and fluctuating gas prices. Finally, depreciation is the loss in value of your car over time, affected by its make, model, age, and condition. All these factors combined give you a realistic view of what owning a car will truly cost, helping you budget effectively.

Choosing the right car is about balancing what you need with what you can afford. Consider how you plan to use the car: Do you need something fuel-efficient for long commutes or perhaps a larger vehicle for carrying sports equipment or musical instruments? Reliability should be a top priority, as frequent breakdowns can be costly and inconvenient. Safety is another critical factor, especially if you'll be driving younger siblings around. Research cars that have strong safety ratings and the latest security features. New cars generally come with more advanced safety features and warranties that cover repairs for a certain period, but they're also more expensive and depreciate faster. Used cars can be of great value, especially models known for their durability, but it's important to get a comprehensive history and possibly a mechanic's inspection before buying.

When it comes to negotiating, knowledge is your best tool. Research the market value of the car you're interested in, using resources like Kelley Blue Book or Edmunds, to understand what a fair price looks like. Visit multiple dealerships or sellers to compare prices and don't be afraid to haggle. Understanding dealer margins—the difference between what the dealer paid for the car and their selling price—can give you the upper hand in negotiations. Timing can also play a role; dealerships often have quotas to meet at the end of the month, quarter, or year and may offer better deals to boost their sales figures.

Financing a car is another aspect where your prior research and understanding of credit come into play. Various financing options are available, including bank loans, financing through a dealership, or leasing. Each has its pros and cons. Bank loans often have lower interest rates but might require a down payment. Dealership financing can be more convenient and sometimes offers promotional interest rates, but be wary of high fees or inflated rates. Leasing can be appealing due to lower monthly payments and the ability to drive a new car every few years, but it comes with restrictions like mileage limits. You also won't own the car at the end of the lease. A good credit score and a solid down payment can significantly improve your financing terms, reducing the overall cost of owning the car.

Understanding these aspects of buying and owning a car prepares you financially and empowers you to make decisions that align with your personal and financial goals. Whether you opt for a new or used vehicle, negotiate your way to a fair deal, or choose the best financing option, each step you take is an important part of your journey toward responsible car ownership. Remember, a car is not just a means of transportation; it's a financial commitment that, when managed wisely, can serve you well without straining your budget.

7.3 PLANNING FOR STUDY ABROAD: BUDGETING FOR THE BIG TRIP

Imagine stepping off a plane, ready to immerse yourself in a new country, culture, and educational environment. Studying abroad is an exhilarating prospect that broadens your horizons and deepens your academic and personal growth. However, such an adventure requires careful financial planning to ensure it enriches rather than strains your finances. Let's navigate through the various costs and strategize on how to manage and fund this transformative experience.

When you plan your study abroad, think beyond just the tuition fees. Your budget should encompass all aspects of your stay: travel costs, accommodation, daily living expenses, and often overlooked, but crucial emergency funds and healthcare. Travel expenses, including your flight, visa, and travel insurance, can be substantial. Accommodation choices vary widely, from dormitories, which might be cheaper, to private apartments offering more comfort but at a higher cost. Daily living costs will include food, transportation, and leisure activities, which can vary dramatically depending on the country and city. For instance, living in Paris or Tokyo is likely to be significantly more expensive than studying in smaller cities or towns. Additionally, setting aside funds for unexpected expenses like healthcare—where costs can be unpredictable and often high—is essential. This comprehensive budgeting will give you a realistic picture and help prevent any unpleasant financial surprises during your stay.

Funding your study abroad is not just about tapping into savings; it also involves exploring scholarships and grants dedicated to international studies. Many organizations and universities offer scholarships that cover tuition, travel, or living expenses, specifically for students studying abroad. Start your search early, as these opportunities often have early deadlines and require detailed applications, including essays and recommendations. Besides scholarships, consider creative fundraising ideas. Crowdfunding platforms allow you to create a campaign to raise money for your trip. You can also organize community events, such as bake sales or art shows, to fundraise for your journey. These efforts help raise money and build a community of support for your adventures abroad.

Managing your money while living in a different country is a task that demands attention and care. One of the first challenges is dealing with currency exchange rates. Always keep an eye on these rates, as they can fluctuate significantly, affecting your budget. Using reliable currency exchange services and being cautious about transaction fees will help you manage your funds better.

Secure money transfers are another critical aspect. Opt for trusted international transfer services that offer transparency and minimal fees. When it comes to daily spending, using local bank accounts or student cards can reduce costs related to currency conversion. Most importantly, always have a financial backup plan. International credit cards or emergency cash are vital in unexpected situations.

Cultural and financial preparedness go hand in hand when studying abroad. Each country has its unique way of handling money – from cash preferences to tipping norms. Before you go, research these cultural nuances to avoid any faux pas or financial blunders. Budgeting daily expenses can be tricky in a new environment. Start by tracking your spending closely in the first few weeks to set a realistic budget that aligns with local cost levels. This approach helps you manage your finances effectively. It immerses you deeper into the local culture, transforming your financial awareness into a tool for cultural integration.

As you prepare for your study abroad, embracing these financial strategies will ease your transition into a new country and enhance your overall experience. This will allow you to focus on the invaluable experiences and opportunities that lie ahead. With careful planning and a proactive approach, you can navigate the financial aspects of studying abroad as confidently as you explore your new academic and cultural surroundings.

7.4 EMERGENCY FUNDS: WHY AND HOW TO START ONE

Imagine this: you're driving to a friend's house when suddenly your car makes a strange noise and comes to a halt. Or maybe you wake up one day with a fever, and the next thing you know, you're facing a hefty medical bill. These aren't just hypothetical scenarios —they're real-life situations where an emergency fund can be a financial lifesaver. Having money set aside for unexpected expenses is like having a safety net that catches you, preventing a fall into debt that can be hard to climb out of. It's about being prepared, and here, we'll explore why an emergency fund is crucial and how you can build one effectively.

The importance of an emergency fund can't be overstated. Your financial buffer protects you against life's unforeseen costs, which can come at any time without warning. Without it, you might have to rely on credit cards or loans, leading to debt that accrues high interest, complicating your financial life. But with it, you have the ready cash to handle emergencies without disrupting your financial stability or future plans. Think of it as your financial shock absorber—it softens the impact of life's bumps and jolts.

Calculating the right amount for your emergency fund generally involves looking at your total living expenses—rent, food, utilities, and other monthly bills—and aiming to save enough to cover these for three to six months. This range can give you enough breathing room to navigate through most crises, from minor car repairs to more significant issues like losing a job. Start by detailing your monthly expenses, then multiply that by the number of months you feel is right for your situation. If you're still financially dependent on your parents, you might aim for the lower end, but if you're closer to stepping out on your own, you might lean towards six months' worth.

Best practices for saving for an emergency fund focus on consistency and accessibility. Setting up automatic savings can be a game-changer. It involves setting a fixed amount of money to automatically transfer from your checking account to a savings account every month. This method works beautifully because it makes saving non-negotiable, just like paying any other bill. Choosing high-liquidity savings options is also crucial. High-yield savings accounts or money market accounts are ideal because they offer higher interest rates than traditional savings accounts and allow easy access to your funds when needed. Prioritizing contributions to your emergency fund over other non-essential spending can accelerate your progress. Even small contributions can build up over time, turning what might seem like a trickle of savings into a substantial reservoir of financial security.

Maintaining and using the fund wisely is where discipline comes into play. Defining what constitutes an emergency is essential—a true emergency is unexpected and necessary, not just a spontaneous desire for a new gadget or a last-minute vacation. Restrict the use of these funds for real emergencies and avoid dipping into them for everyday expenses. If you do need to use the money, focus on replenishing it as soon as possible. Treat the replenishment just like you treated the initial saving—set up automatic deposits, prioritize the fund in your budget, and adjust your spending to refill what was spent.

Having an emergency fund is more than just a financial recommendation; it's a fundamental aspect of healthy financial management. It empowers you to face life's uncertainties with confidence, knowing that you are prepared to handle challenges without derailing your financial goals. As you build and maintain your emergency fund, you cultivate financial security and peace of mind, which is priceless.

This discussion on emergency funds wraps up our exploration in Chapter 7, where we've tackled some of the most significant financial undertakings you might face—from funding higher education and purchasing your first car to planning an enriching study abroad experience. Each of these scenarios requires careful planning and financial foresight, and the strategies outlined here aim to equip you with the tools you need to approach these challenges with confidence and clarity. As we close this chapter, remember that each step you take in planning for these significant expenses prepares you for these big moments and strengthens your overall financial acumen. Our next chapter will delve into protecting yourself financially, where we'll explore how to safeguard your financial future against potential risks and uncertainties.

CHAPTER EIGHT

PROTECTING YOURSELF FINANCIALLY

Have you ever felt that uneasy shiver down your spine when you hear stories of people getting tricked out of their hard-earned money? It's a cold reminder that the financial world, while full of opportunities, has its fair share of pitfalls, especially for young folks like you who are just beginning to navigate these waters. This chapter is all about arming you with the knowledge and tools to shield yourself against financial scams, which are sadly all too common in today's digital age. Think of this as learning self-defense, but instead of protecting your physical self, you're protecting your financial well-being.

8.1 IDENTIFYING AND AVOIDING SCAMS TARGETED AT TEENS

Common Scams Targeting Teens

Scams can come in many disguises, and being young and possibly inexperienced makes you an attractive target for fraudsters. Some of the most common scams you might encounter include phishing attempts, where scammers pretend to be reputable companies to steal personal information. Then, there are fake job offers or scholarship scams, which might promise great opportunities or financial aid in exchange for a fee or sensitive information. For instance, you might see a job advertised online promising high earnings for minimal work, but when you apply, they ask you for a payment to cover 'training materials' or 'insurance'. These are red flags—legitimate jobs will never ask you to pay to start working.

Another prevalent scam is the too-good-to-be-true scholarship that guarantees financial aid, as long as you pay an upfront fee. Remember, genuine scholarships do not require fees. These scammers prey on the hopes of students looking to secure their educational future, only to leave them with less money and no actual aid. It's heartbreaking and frustrating, but being aware is the first step to protecting yourself.

Red Flags and Warning Signs

Let's talk about some warning signs that can help you sniff out a scam before it's too late. High-pressure tactics are a common strategy used by scammers. They might try to rush you into making decisions, often insisting that an offer is "limited-time" or "once in a lifetime." They know that, given time, you might see through their deception. Always take your time to research and think decisions through, especially when they involve your finances.

Requests for personal information, such as your banking details or passwords, should always be met with skepticism. Legitimate organizations understand the protocols of data protection and will not ask you to share sensitive information through insecure platforms like email or over the phone. Offers that seem too good to be true, like an iPhone for a fraction of the market price, are almost always scams. Trust your gut— if something feels off, it probably is.

Preventive Measures

Protecting yourself requires proactive measures. Always verify the legitimacy of an offer or company before engaging with them. This can be as simple as a Google search, checking reviews, or looking up the company on websites like the Better Business Bureau. Please educate yourself about the common scams and stay updated on new ones, as scammers continually evolve their strategies. Another effective preventive strategy is to discuss opportunities that involve money with a trusted adult—sometimes, a second opinion can offer new insights and save you from potential fraud.

Action Steps if Scammed

If you suspect that you've been scammed, acting quickly can minimize the damage. The first step is to contact your bank or credit card company to report the suspicion and possibly halt any unauthorized transactions. Change your passwords immediately, especially if you suspect that your information might have been compromised. Reporting the scam to authorities can also help prevent others from falling victim to the same fraud. In the U.S., the Federal Trade Commission (FTC) is a good place to start. Keep all evidence of the scam, such as emails or messages, as they might be useful during the investigation.

By understanding the landscape of financial scams and equipping yourself with knowledge and the right strategies, you can effectively protect your financial future. Remember, in the financial world, being cautious is not a sign of mistrust but of smart maneuvering. Stay vigilant, stay informed, and always step forward with confidence, knowing you're well-prepared to defend your finances against those looking to take advantage.

8.2 INSURANCE BASICS: WHAT TEENS NEED TO KNOW

Navigating the world of insurance might seem like a daunting task, especially when you're just stepping into the responsibilities that come with adulthood. But understanding insurance is like having a safety net under your high-wire act in the circus of life—it's about having peace of mind. So, let's break down what insurance is, why it's crucial, and how you can make informed choices about the policies you might need as a teen.

In its simplest form, insurance is a way of protection from financial loss. It's a form of risk management, primarily used to hedge against the risk of a contingent or uncertain loss. For you, as a teen, certain types of insurance are particularly relevant. Health insurance, for instance, covers medical expenses, which can be crucial in case of an illness or injury. Auto insurance is essential if you're driving; it covers car damages or injuries to other drivers in case of an accident. Then there's personal property insurance, which can cover the cost of your belongings, like your laptop or bicycle, in case they're stolen or damaged.

To understand how insurance works, let's use the example of auto insurance, something you might consider if you're driving. When you buy an auto insurance policy, you pay a premium, which is the amount you pay your insurance company to keep the policy active. This premium varies depending on several factors, including the type of coverage, the likelihood of you making a claim, and the value of the items insured. In exchange for your premium, the insurance company agrees to pay for certain expenses and losses that are covered under your policy, known as your coverage.

Let's say you're involved in a car accident that was your fault, and there's damage to both your car and the other driver's car. Here's where your insurance kicks in. You'll likely have to pay a deductible, which is the amount you pay out of pocket for the damages, before your insurance covers the rest. For example, if your deductible is $500 and the repair costs are $2,000, you pay $500, and your insurance company pays $1,500. The limits of your coverage depend on the terms of your policy; they dictate the maximum amount your insurance company will pay for a single accident.

Choosing the right insurance policy involves comparing different policies to see what coverage they offer and at what cost. This isn't just about finding the cheapest option; it's about finding where you get the most value. It's crucial to read the fine print and understand what is and isn't covered. For instance, some auto insurance policies might offer roadside assistance as part of the package, which can be a lifesaver if your car breaks down. Others might cover rental car costs if your car is in the shop after an accident.

Since insurance terminology can often seem like a foreign language, let's demystify some common terms you'll encounter. Premiums, as you know now, are what you pay periodically to maintain your insurance. The policy limit is the maximum amount an insurance company will pay under a policy for a covered loss. Deductibles are what you pay out of pocket before the insurance pays out. These terms are crucial in understanding how much you'll need to pay in case of an accident or issue, and how much you can expect to be reimbursed.

Understanding these basics of insurance not only prepares you for the practical aspects of managing risks but also helps you make informed decisions about the types of coverage you might need.

Whether it's choosing the right health insurance plan that covers your medical needs or selecting an auto insurance policy that provides adequate coverage while being cost-effective, the knowledge you gain now will serve you throughout your life, ensuring that you can face the uncertainties with confidence.

8.3 SAFEGUARDING YOUR ONLINE BANKING

In the digital age, where almost everything can be done with a click or a tap, managing your finances online has become the norm rather than the exception. It's convenient, fast, and gives you real-time access to your financial life. However, this convenience also comes with its share of risks. Cyber threats are real and can have severe consequences if you're not vigilant. That's why it's crucial to adopt safe online banking practices that protect your financial information from unauthorized access or fraud.

Creating strong passwords is your first line of defense in safeguarding your online banking accounts. A strong password is like a complex lock that is difficult for hackers to open. It should be a mix of letters, numbers, and symbols, and ideally, it should be unique to each account to prevent a domino effect if one account is compromised. Avoid using easily guessable passwords such as birthdays, your name, or sequential numbers. To manage multiple complex passwords, consider using a reputable password manager. These tools can generate and store strong passwords for you and protect them with encryption, ensuring that remembering your passwords doesn't become a juggling act.

Regularly updating software on your devices also plays a critical role in online security. Whether it's your smartphone, tablet, or computer, ensuring that the operating system and applications are up-to-date is essential. Software updates often include patches for security vulnerabilities that have been discovered since the last update. Keeping your software current closes these vulnerabilities, making it harder for cybercriminals to exploit them. Make it a habit to install updates as soon as they become available, or set your devices to update automatically so you don't have to worry about missing an important security enhancement.

When using online banking, always avoid public Wi-Fi networks. Public Wi-Fi is inherently insecure, and using it to access your bank accounts can expose your financial information to anyone else on the same network who might have nefarious intentions. If you need to access your bank account while on the go, use your phone's cellular network, which is more secure, or use a virtual private network (VPN). A VPN encrypts your internet connection, making it secure even when you're using public Wi-Fi.

Monitoring your bank accounts regularly is another key practice in safeguarding your financial health. Most banks offer a variety of alerts that you can set up to monitor account activities. You can choose to receive notifications for transactions above a certain amount, log-ins from new devices, or changes to your account information. These alerts keep you informed of any activity in your account, allowing you to quickly spot and address unauthorized transactions. Regular monitoring helps catch fraud early and keeps you closely connected with your financial transactions, enhancing your overall financial awareness.

Multi-Factor Authentication

In addition to these practices, multi-factor authentication (MFA) is a robust security measure that adds an extra layer of protection to your online banking accounts. MFA requires more than one form of verification to prove your identity when logging into an account, which means simply knowing your password isn't enough for someone to access your account. Typically, MFA involves something you know (like a password), something you have (like a smartphone), and something you are (like a fingerprint).

Setting up MFA can usually be done through your bank's website or app. Once activated, it works like this: you'll enter your username and password as usual, and then you'll be prompted to provide the second form of verification. It might be a code sent to your phone via text message or an app, or it might use a biometric method like fingerprint recognition. This process might seem like a small inconvenience, but it significantly strengthens your account security by ensuring that even if someone has stolen your password, they still can't access your account.

What to Do in Case of Fraud

Despite all precautions, if you suspect that your online banking account has been compromised, take immediate action to limit damage and protect your financial assets. First, contact your bank to report the suspected fraud. This step is crucial, as banks have protocols in place to secure your account, such as freezing it or monitoring it for further unusual activities.

Next, change your online banking passwords immediately. If you've used the same password on other accounts, change those as well. This prevents the fraud from spreading to other areas of your digital life.

Finally, file a report with the relevant authorities. In the United States, you can report online banking fraud to the Internet Crime Complaint Center (IC3) or the Federal Trade Commission (FTC). Reporting helps you recover any financial losses and contributes to a broader effort to combat online fraud.

By adopting these practices and knowing the steps to take in case of fraud, you empower yourself to navigate the digital banking landscape safely and confidently. Remember, the goal here is to protect your money and ensure that your journey into financial independence is secure and prosperous.

8.4 INTELLECTUAL PROPERTY AND MONEY: PROTECTING YOUR CREATIONS

Imagine you've created something unique—a catchy tune on your guitar, a digital artwork, or even an innovative gadget idea. These aren't just cool items to share with friends; they hold value, potentially even a monetary one. This is where understanding intellectual property (IP) becomes crucial. IP is a legal concept that grants you certain protections and rights over the creations of your mind. Essentially, it's about protecting your creative and innovative work from being used without your permission, ensuring that you're the one benefiting if there's money to be made from your creation.

Understanding Intellectual Property

Intellectual property rights come in various forms, each serving different types of creations. Copyrights protect artistic works like music, literature, and art. They automatically apply when you create something original and fix it in a physical form, like writing down lyrics or saving a digital painting on your computer. Trademarks protect symbols, names, and slogans used to identify goods or services—it's what helps distinguish brands in the marketplace. Patents are all about inventions; they give you exclusive rights to make, use, or sell your invention for a certain period, typically 20 years from the filing date. Understanding these types of protections helps you navigate how to secure and defend your rights, ensuring that your creative outputs are safeguarded.

Monetizing IP

Turning your creative skills into an income stream might sound daunting, but it's entirely feasible with the right approach. Licensing your music to be used in commercials, video games, or as background tracks for YouTube videos can generate royalties each time your music is used. Selling digital art through online platforms can also provide continuous income if you retain the copyright over your work and sell copies or prints. If you've invented something, patenting it can secure your exclusive rights, allowing you to manufacture it yourself or license the technology to others. These avenues bring financial benefits and bolster your professional reputation as a creator.

Protecting IP Legally

But how do you ensure your intellectual property is protected? First, understanding the registration process is crucial. Copyright registration can be done through your country's copyright office, offering legal proof of your ownership and the date of creation. Trademarks require a bit more groundwork; you need to ensure your brand name or logo isn't already in use and then register it to prevent others from using similar marks. Patenting an invention involves a detailed application describing your invention in technical terms, proving it's novel. For all these processes, seeking professional legal advice can be invaluable. Intellectual property law is complex, and a knowledgeable expert can help navigate the intricacies, ensuring your creations are protected.

Dealing with IP Theft

Discovering that someone else is using your creation without permission can be deeply unsettling. If you believe your intellectual property has been stolen or misused, the first step is to gather evidence—screenshots, records of your original work, and any correspondence related to the infringement. With this information, you can issue a cease-and-desist letter, a formal request for the infringer to stop using your creation. If the issue escalates, legal action may be necessary. Here again, consulting with an intellectual property attorney can guide you through the process, helping you defend your rights and potentially recover losses.

Handling intellectual property wisely secures your creations and opens doors to new opportunities and financial benefits. Whether you're a budding artist, an aspiring musician, or a young inventor, understanding and leveraging IP rights can transform your innovative ideas into valuable assets. As you continue to explore and create, keep these principles in mind, ensuring that your intellectual and creative contributions are properly protected and rewarding.

As we wrap up this exploration of protecting yourself financially, remember that each concept, from recognizing scams to safeguarding your intellectual creations, contributes to building a secure financial foundation. These strategies empower you to confidently navigate the financial landscape, fully prepared to protect and maximize your assets. Up next, we'll dive into the world of credit, exploring how it works and how you can use it to your advantage. Stay tuned for these enlightening insights that will further equip you to make informed financial decisions.

CHAPTER NINE

NAVIGATING THE DIGITAL FINANCIAL WORLD

Imagine stepping into a vast, bustling city where every street and corner is brimming with opportunities to learn, grow, and manage your finances with just a click or a tap. This is the digital financial world, a place that might seem overwhelming at first glance but is packed with tools designed to enhance your financial freedom and competence. As you navigate this modern landscape, you'll discover that mastering the art of online banking is much like learning to ride a bike in this bustling city—intimidating at first, but liberating once you know how to navigate it.

9.1 MASTERING ONLINE BANKING: TIPS AND TRICKS

Getting Started with Online Banking

Diving into online banking can be as exciting as opening a treasure chest, but the real treasure is the convenience and control it offers over your finances. First, choosing the right bank is crucial. Look for banks that offer robust online features that cater specifically to your needs as a teen. These might include user-friendly interfaces, minimal fees, and resources tailored to help you understand the nuances of financial management. When setting up your online banking account, you'll typically need some basic information: your Social Security number, a valid I.D., and proof of address. Most banks now allow you to set up an account fully online, making it convenient to start right from home.

Once your account is set up, take some time to familiarize yourself with the dashboard and various features. Most online banking platforms will enable you to check your balance, view transaction history, transfer money between accounts, and pay bills online. These functions save you trips to the bank and give you real-time insights into your financial status, which is invaluable for making informed financial decisions.

Features and Benefits

One of the most transformative features of online banking is the ability to make electronic transfers and mobile deposits. Imagine you're at a coffee shop with friends and need to split the bill. Instead of dealing with cash, you can simply transfer your share to your friend's account using your mobile banking app. Likewise, if you receive a check as a gift, there's no need to rush to the bank. Just snap a picture of the check through your banking app and deposit it straight into your account. These features not only add layers of convenience but also help you manage your finances more efficiently and securely.

Another significant benefit is real-time account monitoring. This feature allows you to see exactly where your money is going at any moment, which is especially useful for quickly budgeting and spotting unauthorized transactions. Many banks also offer customizable alerts, which can notify you of low balances, unusual activity, or upcoming bills, helping you avoid overdraft fees and fraud.

Security Best Practices

As you embrace the advantages of online banking, it's critical to navigate this digital city with caution, especially when it concerns security. Always use strong, unique passwords for your banking accounts, and consider using a password manager to keep track of them. Activate two-factor authentication (2FA) for an added layer of security. This typically involves receiving a code on your phone that you must enter along with your password when logging in.

Be vigilant about phishing attempts and fraudulent communications. These are usually emails or messages that try to trick you into giving away your personal information. Remember, a legitimate bank will never ask for sensitive information through email or text messages. If you receive something suspicious, contact your bank directly using a phone number from their official website, not the one provided in the suspicious email.

Troubleshooting Common Issues

Even in the most streamlined systems, issues can arise. Common problems like forgotten passwords, locked accounts, or errors in transactions are usually easy to resolve. Most banks offer online resources for resetting passwords or unlocking accounts. If you encounter a transaction error, documenting the details and promptly contacting customer support can help resolve the issue. Most banks are equipped to handle these inquiries and can often rectify problems quickly.

Navigating the digital financial world with confidence comes from understanding and leveraging the tools at your disposal. Online banking, with its extensive features and benefits, offers a powerful way to manage your finances effectively and securely. As you continue to explore and utilize these tools, you'll find that managing your money online is not just a convenience but a significant step towards financial independence and savvy.

9.2 CRYPTOCURRENCY: BASICS FOR TEENS

Imagine stepping into a digital realm where traditional money—those physical bills and coins you're used to handling—is replaced by digital tokens that exist entirely online. This realm isn't a futuristic fantasy; it's the world of cryptocurrencies, a fascinating intersection of finance and technology, becoming increasingly relevant in our digital age. Cryptocurrencies are essentially digital or virtual currencies that use cryptography for security, making them difficult to counterfeit. Unlike traditional currencies, they are decentralized and typically based on blockchain technology. This is a distributed ledger that is enforced by a disparate network of computers.

A blockchain is like a continuously growing list of records, called blocks, which are linked securely together. Each block contains a cryptographic hash of the previous block, a timestamp, and transaction data, making the entire process secure and transparent. This technology supports cryptocurrency transactions and ensures their integrity and reliability. The appeal of cryptocurrencies, such as Bitcoin, Ethereum, and Litecoin, lies in their ability to provide a secure, private, and global way to store and exchange value without the need for intermediaries like banks or governments.

Bitcoin, the first cryptocurrency, was created in 2009 as an alternative to traditional currencies because it has lower transaction fees than traditional online payment. In addition, it is operated by a decentralized authority, which is different from government-issued currencies. Ethereum, launched in 2015, goes a step further by enabling developers to create and deploy smart contracts—self-executing contracts with the terms directly written into code. Litecoin, often referred to as the 'silver to Bitcoin's gold,' was introduced in 2011 and offers faster processing times and a higher number of maximum coins.

These cryptocurrencies have introduced a new way of thinking about money and created a dynamic, albeit volatile, investment landscape. The value of cryptocurrencies can rapidly increase or decrease over a short time due to factors like technological changes, market demand, and investor sentiment. This volatility can be both a risk and an opportunity. On one hand, the rapid price increase can result in significant gains for investors; on the other, the sudden downturns can lead to equally substantial losses.

RISKS AND REWARDS

Investing in cryptocurrencies is not without its risks. The same volatility that can lead to high returns can also result in substantial losses. Furthermore, regulatory changes can significantly impact the value of cryptocurrencies. Governments worldwide are still figuring out how to deal with cryptocurrencies, and their legal stance can affect their usability and acceptance. Additionally, while the technology behind cryptocurrencies—blockchain—is secure, the exchanges and wallets where cryptocurrencies are bought, sold, and stored can be vulnerable to hacking.

Despite these risks, the potential benefits of cryptocurrencies and the technology behind them—particularly blockchain—are significant. Blockchain technology offers a level of security and transparency in transactions that traditional financial systems struggle to match. For you, as a teen, understanding this technology and its potential implications for the future digital economy could be incredibly valuable, whether or not you choose to invest in cryptocurrencies.

GETTING STARTED SAFELY

If you're considering dipping your toes into the world of cryptocurrencies, start by educating yourself thoroughly. Understand the technology, the specific currency, and the market conditions. When you're ready to invest, choose a reputable exchange. Exchanges like Coinbase, Binance, and Kraken have established themselves as trustworthy platforms with robust security measures. However, it's crucial to use strong, unique passwords and enable two-factor authentication to safeguard your accounts.

Storing your cryptocurrencies safely is equally important. While exchanges are convenient for buying and selling, they can be vulnerable to hacks. Using a cryptocurrency wallet—a software program or physical device that stores the keys you use to send and receive various cryptocurrencies—can provide an extra layer of security. There are two main types of wallets: hot wallets, which are connected to the internet and more convenient for frequent trading, and cold wallets, which are not connected to the internet and are better for long-term storage of larger amounts.

Understanding private keys—cryptographic keys that allow you to access your cryptocurrency—is crucial. These keys are what you use to prove ownership of your digital assets and to execute transactions. If lost, you could permanently lose access to your cryptocurrency. Therefore, keeping your private keys secure and backed up is essential.

Navigating the world of cryptocurrencies can be thrilling and enlightening. As you explore this digital financial frontier, remember the importance of cautious exploration. Equip yourself with knowledge, understand the risks and rewards, and proceed with a strategy that respects both the potentials and drawbacks of these digital assets.

9.3 FINANCIAL APPS: WHAT'S AVAILABLE FOR TEENS?

Navigating the digital financial landscape can sometimes feel like exploring a vast, bustling marketplace, where every stall and shop promises tools and solutions that can make managing your money simpler and more efficient. As a teen stepping into this world, you might find an array of financial apps designed specifically with your needs in mind—apps that cater to budgeting, saving, investing, and tracking expenses. These apps are not just about keeping tabs on your money; they offer a way to make financial management an integral and seamless part of your daily life.

Let's explore a curated list of user-friendly financial apps that are particularly well-suited to you as a teen. Consider 'Credit Karma', a popular budgeting app that helps you track your spending and stay on top of your financial goals. It automatically categorizes your transactions from linked credit and debit cards and displays them in easy-to-understand charts. This visualization helps you see exactly where your money goes each month, whether it's meals out with friends, new video games, or savings towards college. Another great tool is 'YNAB' (You Need A Budget), which adopts a unique approach to budgeting that focuses on giving every dollar a job. It encourages proactive financial planning, such as setting aside money for upcoming expenses, which can be particularly helpful for managing irregular income from part-time jobs or freelance gigs.

When evaluating which financial app to integrate into your routine, consider several key features that enhance their utility.

The user interface, for instance, is crucial. An app with a clean, intuitive interface is easier to navigate and will be more engaging to use regularly. Security measures are paramount as well. Look for apps that offer encrypted data storage, two-factor authentication, and other security protocols that protect your financial information from unauthorized access. Also, consider the cost—many apps offer free basic services with options to upgrade for more features. Lastly, the ability to sync with your bank accounts and other financial tools can provide a more holistic view of your finances, making the app a one-stop shop for all your financial needs.

To help you choose the best app to meet your financial management needs, it's beneficial to consider reviews and recommendations from other users and financial experts. For instance, apps like 'Acorns' and 'Stash' are often recommended for beginners interested in investing. They allow you to start with small amounts and offer educational resources that demystify investment concepts. User reviews can highlight both these apps' strengths and potential drawbacks, giving you a clearer picture of how they might fit into your lifestyle and financial goals.

Understanding app permissions and privacy settings is crucial in protecting your personal information. Many apps require access to your financial data to function effectively. It's essential to understand what data the app collects, how it is used, and how it is protected. Ensure the app's privacy policy is transparent and aligns with your comfort levels regarding data sharing. Adjust app settings to limit unnecessary data access or sharing, and be wary of apps that require overly broad permissions as a condition of use.

By incorporating these digital tools into your financial routine, you can take significant strides toward becoming more aware, proactive, and confident in managing your money. Whether it's saving for a new laptop, budgeting for weekly expenses, or starting to invest, these apps provide you with the resources to achieve your financial goals with a level of independence and competence that sets the foundation for a secure financial future. Keep exploring, learning, and adapting the tools and practices that resonate with your personal and financial growth aspirations.

9.4 THE ROLE OF SOCIAL MEDIA IN FINANCIAL DECISIONS

In today's digital age, social media isn't just a platform for connecting with friends; it's become a significant player in shaping financial behaviors and decisions, especially for teens like you. Scrolling through your feeds, it's easy to see how Instagram, TikTok, and other platforms can subtly (and not so subtly) influence your spending habits. Using sophisticated algorithms, targeted advertising serves up ads that perfectly match your interests and previous search histories. These ads can be incredibly persuasive, presenting products as 'must-haves' and creating a sense of urgency with limited-time offers. This can lead to impulse buys, where the emotional thrill of snagging a deal overtakes the practical consideration of whether you really need or can afford the item.

Peer pressure plays a significant role as well. Seeing friends and influencers flaunt the latest gadgets, fashion, or exotic vacations can stir feelings of envy and a desire to keep up. It's a phenomenon often referred to as 'keeping up with the digital Joneses,' where the online showcase of others' spending can skew your perception of everyday spending and lifestyle standards. This digital peer pressure can make it challenging to stick to a budget or save for future goals, as the immediate gratification of online purchases is always just a few clicks away.

However, it's not all doom and gloom. Social media also offers substantial benefits, especially regarding financial education and literacy. Many financial experts and educators use these platforms to share valuable information, offering everything from basic budgeting tips to more complex investment strategies. Engaging with these resources can turn your feed into a classroom, where learning about finances becomes as accessible and entertaining as checking in on your friends' latest posts. For instance, following hashtags like #PersonalFinance or #FinancialFreedom can lead you to a wealth of posts and videos dedicated to improving financial knowledge.

When following financial influencers, it's crucial to discern between credible sources and those just selling a dream. Look for influencers who back up their advice with verifiable facts and who disclose their affiliations with financial products or services. Be skeptical of those promising quick riches or guaranteed returns, as these are common red flags for misleading or fraudulent advice. Instead, focus on those who offer balanced, well-reasoned insights and encourage responsible financial behaviors. Always cross-verify the tips you receive with other trusted sources before making financial decisions based on social media advice.

Managing your digital footprint is another critical aspect of engaging with social media, especially involving financial content. Remember, the posts you interact with, the comments you make, and the information you share can all be traced back to you. This digital trail can have implications for your privacy and future opportunities. For example, potential employers or colleges might review your social media presence, and overt displays of irresponsible spending or poor financial decisions could impact their perceptions of you. To safeguard your online reputation, adjust your privacy settings to control who can see your posts and interactions. Be mindful of the information you share, especially when discussing finances or personal purchases.

In essence, while social media can influence your spending in ways that might not always benefit your financial health, it also offers tools and opportunities for improving your financial knowledge and decision-making. By approaching social media with a critical eye, you can harness its power to enhance, rather than undermine, your financial stability. This balanced approach to digital engagement ensures that social media remains a valuable part of your financial education toolkit, empowering you to make informed decisions that support your long-term financial goals.

As we close this chapter on navigating the digital financial world, remember the dual role social media can play. It can be a gateway to impulse spending or a portal to financial wisdom. The choice of which path to follow is yours. Armed with the knowledge and strategies discussed, you're better equipped to use digital tools responsibly and to your advantage. Up next, we'll explore ethical and responsible finance, diving into how your financial decisions can align with your values and impact the world around you.

CHAPTER TEN

ETHICAL AND RESPONSIBLE FINANCE

Imagine you're at a crossroads where every path you take can make a significant difference—not just in your life but in the world around you. This is the essence of ethical and responsible finance. It's about making choices that reflect your values and aspirations, and recognizing that your financial decisions have the power to shape a better world. In this chapter, we'll navigate the rewarding path of Socially Responsible Investing (SRI), a strategy that marries your financial goals with your personal convictions about what is good for society and the environment.

10.1 SOCIALLY RESPONSIBLE INVESTING: MAKING MONEY WHILE DOING GOOD

Understanding Socially Responsible Investing (SRI)

Socially Responsible Investing (SRI) isn't just about avoiding investments in industries that conflict with your values, like tobacco or firearms; it's about proactively contributing to advancements in social, environmental, and governance practices. SRI involves selecting investments based on both financial return and social/environmental good to bring about societal change. This approach can include investing in companies that promote environmental stewardship, consumer protection, human rights, and diversity. Some might believe that this limits your investment options, but in reality, it opens up a new avenue to align your financial growth with your ethical beliefs.

The concept of SRI might seem complex, but at its heart, it's about making sure your money is working for you and the betterment of the world. Think of it as the financial world's version of "voting with your dollar." By choosing where you invest, you're endorsing a set of values, supporting the issues you care about, like renewable energy or ethical labor practices. It's a powerful way to influence global practices while building your wealth.

Evaluating SRI Opportunities

When diving into SRI, the first step is learning how to assess potential investments. This involves more than just looking at financial returns. You'll want to consider your investments' social or environmental impact, which can be evaluated through corporate social responsibility (CSR) reports, third-party SRI ratings, and news sources. These resources can tell you a lot about a company's labor policies, environmental impact, and corporate governance.

When assessing an SRI fund or a company, consider:

- Company policies: What are their policies on environmental sustainability and social responsibility?
- Environmental impact reports: How transparent is the company in reporting its environmental footprint?

- SRI ratings: Financial services often provide ratings based on a company's social and environmental impact.

Make it a habit to look beneath the surface of potential investments to understand the full scope of their business practices. This might require additional effort, but the payoff is investing in financially sound companies that align with your vision of a sustainable future.

Impact of SRI Choices

The impact of SRI is profound and far-reaching. By choosing to invest in responsible companies, you are part of a movement that pressures businesses to improve their practices. For instance, an increase in investment in renewable energy companies can drive down the cost of clean energy, making it more accessible and leading to greater environmental benefits.

Consider the case of a company that started focusing on reducing waste in its manufacturing processes after receiving significant investments from SRI funds. This shift helped the environment and improved the company's efficiency and public image, ultimately increasing its market value. Such examples underscore that SRI isn't just good ethics—it's also good economics.

Getting Started with SRI

Embarking on your SRI journey can be as simple as choosing a mutual fund or an exchange-traded fund (ETF) that aligns with your values. Many financial institutions now offer funds geared explicitly towards environmental sustainability, human rights, or clean energy. Start by researching these options, comparing their performance, fees, and the specific causes they support.

For a hands-on approach, engage in shareholder advocacy. As a shareholder, you can influence company policy through direct dialogue, submitting proposals, and voting on company issues. This active involvement ensures your voice is heard on critical issues, from environmental policies to corporate governance.

Lastly, remember that every investment carries risk, and it's essential to diversify your portfolio. Balancing SRI with other investment strategies can protect your financial future while still allowing you to support the causes important to you. Tools like online investment platforms and robo-advisors can provide guidance on creating a diversified SRI portfolio that matches your risk tolerance and financial goals.

Incorporating SRI into your investment strategy is not just about growing your wealth; it's about making a difference with your dollars. It's a testament to the power of mindful investing—where every choice can contribute to a larger good, reinforcing the idea that what is beneficial for the world can also be beneficial for your wallet. By investing responsibly, you're paving the way for a future where finance and values go hand in hand—creating a legacy of positive impact that goes beyond mere monetary gains.

10.2 THE IMPACT OF YOUR FINANCIAL DECISIONS ON THE ENVIRONMENT

Carbon Footprint of Spending

Every time you spend money, you're not just buying a product or a service; you're also casting a vote for the kind of world you want to live in. The concept of a carbon footprint, which measures the total greenhouse gas emissions caused directly and indirectly by a person or organization, can be applied to your spending habits as well. For instance, when you purchase a new t-shirt, you're not just paying for the fabric and the design, but also for the carbon footprint of the entire production process—from the cultivation of cotton, through manufacturing, all the way to the transportation of the final product to the store.

The fashion industry, for example, is one of the largest polluters globally, second only to oil. It's a sobering fact that might make you think twice about buying that extra pair of jeans. Similarly, the technology industry, while innovative, contributes significantly to environmental degradation through mining for rare earth elements and generating considerable electronic waste. Even the food industry has its stakes in environmental impact, with meat and dairy production accounting for a significant portion of agricultural greenhouse gas emissions.

Understanding these connections might feel overwhelming, but it also empowers you to make choices that align more closely with your environmental values. Simple actions like choosing quality over quantity or opting for products made with sustainable practices can significantly reduce your personal carbon footprint. It's about seeing the bigger picture and realizing that every purchase has hidden costs and consequences.

Eco-friendly Financial Habits

Adopting eco-friendly financial habits is like turning the tide in small but significant ways. One straightforward change is going digital wherever possible—opt for online statements and bills instead of paper ones, use digital tickets and boarding passes, and read online instead of buying physical books and magazines. These actions reduce paper waste and the energy associated with paper production, transportation, and disposal.

Another impactful habit is using energy-efficient appliances. Look for products with the Energy Star label, which signifies that the appliance uses less energy than traditional models. This helps reduce your carbon footprint and save money on utility bills. Additionally, support businesses that have green certifications. These businesses take steps to minimize their environmental impact, and by patronizing them, you help to encourage more companies to follow in their footsteps.

Investing in renewable energy and green technologies supports the growth of environmentally friendly practices and positions you to benefit from the shift toward sustainability. As the world increasingly moves away from fossil fuels, renewable energy sources like solar and wind are becoming more cost-effective and widespread. Investing in these technologies does not only contribute to a healthier planet but can also offer substantial returns as demand continues to grow.

Lifecycle of Products

Every product goes through a lifecycle—from raw material extraction to production, distribution, use, and disposal. Each stage of this lifecycle has environmental implications, and being aware of these can guide you to make more sustainable choices. For instance, opting for products with a longer lifespan reduces the demand for frequent manufacturing and ultimately results in less waste. Choosing products that are recyclable or made from recycled materials can also have a significant impact by reducing the need for new raw materials and decreasing waste.

Moreover, consider the end of a product's life. Opting for biodegradable or recyclable items means they are less likely to clog landfills. For example, when buying electronics, look for brands that offer recycling programs for their products or choose furniture made from natural materials that can be more easily recycled or even composted.

In essence, each financial decision you make sends ripples through the environment, affecting your immediate surroundings and the global ecosystem. By making informed choices—whether it's what you buy, where you invest, or how you dispose of used products—you are taking responsibility for your slice of the impact on our planet. Your actions, no matter how small, can contribute to a collective effort toward a more sustainable and equitable world.

10.3 ETHICAL SHOPPING: HOW YOUR PURCHASES AFFECT OTHERS

When you stand in a store, gazing at shelves lined with vibrant packages, do you ever pause and wonder where each product came from? Who made it, and what was their life like? This is the heart of ethical consumerism—a practice that encourages you to make purchase decisions that consider the product's full backstory, particularly the welfare of people and animals, and the environmental impact involved in its production. Ethical consumerism isn't just about avoiding products that don't align with your values; it's about actively choosing to support businesses and practices that do good by their workers, animals, and the planet.

Understanding ethical consumerism begins with recognizing how everyday purchases can contribute to or help alleviate issues like unfair labor practices, animal cruelty, and environmental damage. Each dollar you spend can be a vote towards a more ethical world. For instance, buying a chocolate bar might seem simple, but when you choose a brand that uses ethically sourced cocoa, you are supporting fair labor practices and helping to reduce exploitation in the cocoa supply chains. This conscious decision-making process doesn't have to be overwhelming—it can start with small, manageable steps that gradually build into a lifestyle.

Identifying ethical brands can sometimes feel like searching for a needle in a haystack, especially when marketing jargon and greenwashing—a practice where companies convey a false impression of their products being environmentally sound—are rampant. However, learning to look for certain labels and certifications can make this easier. Look for fair trade certifications, organic labels, or cruelty-free logos, as these often indicate higher ethical standards. Additionally, diving a bit deeper by reading up on a company's corporate social responsibility (CSR) reports can reveal their commitments and practices regarding social and environmental issues. These reports can usually be found on the company's website and will provide insight into its operations and values.

The power of consumer demand in shaping corporate behavior cannot be underestimated. Historically, consumer advocacy has led to significant changes in business practices. For example, the push from buyers for cruelty-free products has prompted many companies to adopt more humane practices and seek cruelty-free certifications. Similarly, the demand for more sustainable packaging has led some companies to innovate with biodegradable or recyclable materials. You, as a consumer, have more power than you might think. By choosing to spend your money on products and services that align with your ethical views, you help push industries toward more sustainable and humane practices.

To make ethical shopping more accessible and practical, start by prioritizing local and fair-trade products. Shopping locally supports small businesses in your community and often means a lower carbon footprint due to reduced transportation distances. Fair-trade products, while sometimes more expensive, ensure that producers receive a fair price for their goods, which can help improve communities and make industries more sustainable. Participating in the sharing economy is another practical step. This could mean anything from borrowing tools instead of buying new ones, using clothing swaps, or participating in library systems. These actions help reduce waste and promote a more circular economy where resources are used more efficiently and responsibly.

Moreover, reducing waste is a significant part of ethical consumerism. Consider the lifecycle of each product you buy. Is it something you will use long-term, or will it end up in the trash after a few uses? Opting for products with minimal packaging or recycled materials can significantly reduce your environmental impact. Remember, each choice you make sends a message about the world you want to live in. By making informed decisions, you contribute to a market that values fairness, sustainability, and compassion. This doesn't just benefit the planet and its inhabitants; it enriches your life, knowing that you are part of a positive change.

10.4 SUPPORTING CAUSES THROUGH FINANCIAL CHOICES

When you think about the concept of philanthropy, you might imagine wealthy individuals donating large sums to prestigious institutions. However, philanthropy isn't just for the affluent; it's an accessible and vital aspect of personal finance for everyone, including you as a young investor. Even small contributions can have a profound impact when directed towards the right causes. It's about leveraging your resources— money, time, or skills—to make a positive difference in the world.

Philanthropy in personal finance is not just about giving away money; it's about strategically using your financial resources to support causes you care about. This could mean donating to a local charity that supports education, funding a community project that aims to clean up the environment, or supporting a nonprofit that works on global health issues. Each dollar you contribute can help these organizations achieve their goals, which in turn helps create a better world. Moreover, engaging in philanthropy can also give you a deeper sense of purpose and connection to your community or the causes you support. It reinforces the idea that your financial decisions can extend beyond personal benefit to societal impact.

Choosing the right causes to support involves thoughtful consideration. Start by reflecting on what matters most to you. Is it the environment, human rights, animal welfare, or perhaps education? Once you've identified your passion areas, research organizations that align with these interests. Look for transparency in how they operate and the effectiveness of their programs. Reputable organizations should have clear information available about their operations, financial health, and program outcomes. Tools like Charity Navigator or GuideStar can provide detailed insights into a charity's performance and financial accountability, helping you make informed decisions about where to allocate your resources.

Integrating charitable giving into your financial planning can be both rewarding and practical. One effective strategy is setting up automatic donations. Many organizations allow you to set up recurring contributions, which can be a convenient way to give. Decide on a percentage of your income or a fixed amount you feel comfortable donating each month. This method ensures that giving becomes a regular part of your budget, just like savings or expenses. Additionally, consider the tax implications of your donations. In many regions, charitable contributions are tax-deductible, which can reduce your taxable income. Keep detailed records of your donations, as these can be valuable during tax season.

While monetary donations are significant, non-monetary contributions can be equally impactful. Volunteering your time or lending your skills to a cause can provide immense value. For instance, if you're a tech-savvy individual, offering to help a nonprofit improve its website can significantly enhance its online presence and operational efficiency. Similarly, participating in community clean-ups or food drives contributes to tangible improvements in your local area. These activities support the organizations and provide rich, hands-on experiences that deepen your understanding of the issues and enhance your personal growth.

In essence, supporting causes through your financial choices is about consciously using your financial and other resources to foster positive change. It's an integral part of building a holistic and impactful approach to personal finance, where success is measured by the wealth you accumulate and the contributions you make towards creating a better world for all.

As we wrap up this exploration into ethical and responsible finance, remember that your financial decisions carry weight far beyond your bank account. They have the power to shape communities, influence industries, and change lives. Let these lessons guide you toward financial success and a life rich with purpose and positive impact. In the next chapter, we'll explore how to prepare for financial independence, a crucial step toward realizing your personal and financial goals in the broader context of the responsible practices we've discussed.

CHAPTER ELEVEN

PREPARING FOR FINANCIAL INDEPENDENCE

Imagine yourself standing at the helm of a ship, the vast ocean ahead filled with possibilities and challenges. As you transition from your teen years to adulthood, financial independence can seem just as vast and daunting. Yet, achieving it is not only empowering but essential for navigating the seas of adult life. This chapter is your compass, guiding you through the essential strategies and knowledge you need to steer your own financial course.

11.1 FROM TEEN TO ADULT: STEPS TOWARD FINANCIAL INDEPENDENCE

Understanding Financial Independence

Financial independence is the milestone where you are able to support yourself without financial assistance from family or other sources. It means having enough income to cover your living expenses and being able to make choices about your life and money without undue stress about finances. This freedom is a powerful goal for many young adults, as it opens up opportunities for choices in life, work, and even further education without being overly burdened by financial constraints.

The journey to financial independence starts with understanding your own finances:

- Knowing how much money you need to live.
- Recognizing where it comes from.
- Managing where it goes.

It's about making informed decisions that align with your personal goals and values, whether that's pursuing higher education, starting a business, or traveling. The essence of financial independence lies in the ability to make choices that fulfill you personally and professionally without being hindered by financial limitations.

Milestones for Financial Independence

Achieving financial independence involves several key milestones. The first is often completing your education, which provides the skills and knowledge necessary to compete in the job market. Securing a steady job follows, which not only provides a regular income but also helps accumulate savings and build wealth. Managing personal finances effectively is another crucial milestone. This includes budgeting, saving, and investing wisely to grow your financial resources.

Another significant milestone is investing in your future. This might mean contributing to a retirement plan, investing in the stock market, or purchasing property. Each of these steps requires different strategies and knowledge, and mastering them can significantly enhance your ability to achieve and maintain financial independence.

Building a Financial Safety Net

One of the foundational steps toward financial independence is establishing a financial safety net. This includes having an emergency fund that can cover at least three to six months of living expenses. Such a fund can be a lifeline in situations like unexpected medical bills, car repairs, or job loss. Starting early to save for this fund and contributing regularly can make a huge difference in your financial security.

Insurance is another crucial aspect of your financial safety net. Understanding and securing the right insurance coverages—whether it's health, auto, or renters insurance—protects you from financial setbacks due to accidents, health issues, or other unforeseen events. Each type of insurance serves a specific purpose, and choosing the right coverage can prevent devastating financial losses.

Transitioning from Parental Support

The transition from relying on parental support to managing your own finances is a significant part of becoming financially independent. This transition often starts with small steps, like taking responsibility for personal expenses such as cellphone bills, car insurance, or personal entertainment costs. Gradually, you can take on more substantial financial responsibilities, like contributing to household bills or managing a credit card.

A strategic approach to this transition involves open communication with your family and/or guardians about financial expectations and responsibilities. It also means setting clear goals for gradually increasing your financial responsibilities and planning how you'll manage these expenses. Tools like budgeting apps or financial tracking software can be extremely helpful in managing your finances as you take on more financial responsibilities.

Visual Element: Interactive Budget Planner

To aid in your journey, consider using an interactive budget planner, such as the one we created in Chapter 7. This tool can help you visualize your income and expenses, making planning and adjusting your budget easier as you take on more financial responsibilities. By inputting different scenarios, you can see how changes in your income or expenses might affect your financial goals, helping you make informed decisions as you move toward financial independence.

Navigating the transition from teen to adult is an exhilarating time, filled with opportunities to shape your financial future. By understanding what financial independence entails and methodically working towards it through clear milestones, building a robust financial safety net, and strategically taking over financial responsibilities, you set the stage for a secure and fulfilling adult life. Remember, each step you take on this path brings you closer to financial autonomy and builds the confidence and skills necessary for lifelong financial wellness.

11.2 NEGOTIATING SALARIES AND BENEFITS FOR YOUR FIRST JOB

Grasping the nuances of salary negotiation and understanding the comprehensive value of job benefits are crucial as you step into the workforce. It's more than just agreeing to a number—it's about recognizing your worth and ensuring you're compensated fairly for your skills and contributions. Let's delve into how you can navigate this important aspect of your career journey with confidence and clarity.

Understanding Your Worth

Before you can effectively negotiate your salary, it's vital to understand what a fair offer looks like in your chosen field. This requires research into industry salary standards, which vary widely depending on the role, your location, and the industry itself. Utilize resources like salary surveys from professional associations, websites like Glassdoor and PayScale, and even job listings in your area to gather data on typical compensation for similar roles. This information serves as a benchmark and empowers you to make informed decisions and negotiations regarding your salary. Furthermore, engaging in discussions on professional networking sites or with mentors in your field can provide insights into salary expectations and negotiation norms. This groundwork equips you with necessary data and boosts your confidence, knowing you're backed by solid research when discussing your salary.

Negotiation Techniques

When the moment arrives to discuss your salary, clarity, and professionalism are your allies. Begin by expressing your enthusiasm for the role and then transition into the negotiation phase by stating your salary expectation clearly, based on the research you've conducted. It's beneficial to provide a range rather than a single figure, which can give you and your employer flexibility while still keeping the discussion within your desired salary bracket. If faced with a lower than anticipated counteroffer, don't shy away from asking how the employer arrived at that number.

This can lead to a constructive discussion about your qualifications and the value you bring to the company.

It is equally important to handle rejections or pushback professionally. If an employer cannot meet your salary expectations, inquire about possibilities for future reviews or increases based on performance. This shows your willingness to prove your worth and your interest in long-term growth within the company. Remember, salary negotiation is a dialogue designed to find mutual ground while respecting both your needs and the constraints of the employer.

Evaluating Job Offers

Receiving a job offer is exciting, but it is crucial to evaluate it comprehensively before accepting. Beyond the salary, consider the benefits package offered, which can significantly affect your overall compensation and job satisfaction. Create a checklist that includes health insurance, retirement plans, paid time off, and other perks like flexible working conditions or professional development opportunities. These benefits can have substantial financial and lifestyle implications. For instance, a robust health insurance plan can save you significant out-of-pocket costs for medical care, while a generous retirement plan can enhance your long-term financial security. Evaluate each element of the offer in light of your personal and professional priorities to make an informed decision.

Importance of:

11.3 MOVING OUT: BUDGETING FOR YOUR FIRST PLACE

Stepping into your own space, whether it's a cozy studio apartment or a shared flat with friends, marks a significant milestone in your life. However, the excitement of this big move should be balanced with a practical understanding of the costs involved. Living independently involves various expenses that go beyond just paying rent. Let's unpack these costs to ensure you're fully prepared to manage them without stress.

Firstly, rent will likely be your largest expense. It's not just a monthly check you write to your landlord, but a commitment that affects your budget significantly. Next, utilities such as electricity, water, gas, and internet are essential services that can vary greatly in cost depending on your usage and the services you choose. It's wise to ask for average utility costs from previous tenants or your landlord to estimate your monthly charges more accurately. Groceries are another critical category. While it might be tempting to eat out frequently, cooking at home can help keep your food expenses under control. Additionally, consider the cost of transportation, whether it involves public transit, fuel for your car, or even occasional rideshares. Each city has its own cost dynamics, and it's crucial to factor in these costs based on your daily commute and lifestyle.

Unforeseen expenses are where many new independents stumble. These could range from a broken microwave that needs replacing to emergency medical expenses not covered by insurance. Setting aside a small monthly amount for such unpredictabilities can prevent financial upheaval. Now, how do we manage all these expenses? Creating a realistic budget is your best tool. Start by listing all your predictable monthly costs, then track your spending over the first few months to identify where you might be overspending or where you can cut back. Budgeting apps or simple spreadsheets can be invaluable for this task, helping you visualize your finances and adjust your spending habits accordingly.

When choosing your first place, the decision between renting and buying is significant and depends largely on your financial stability and long-term plans. Renting offers flexibility, which is excellent if you're still exploring career options or aren't tied to a specific location. On the other hand, buying property is a long-term investment. It can offer financial benefits like building equity and tax deductions. Still, it also comes with added responsibilities and upfront costs such as down payments and maintenance expenses.

Location plays a pivotal role in your housing decision. A place closer to work or college might have higher rent but can save you significant time and transportation costs. Conversely, a less expensive apartment further away might seem like a bargain until you factor in the commute costs and time. If you're considering roommates, choose wisely, as these will be the people you'll coordinate with on rent and utilities, and you'll want to ensure they're reliable and easy to live with. Discuss how bills will be split, the division of household chores, and other shared responsibilities upfront to avoid conflicts later.

Financial Preparation for Moving Out

Moving out for the first time is not just a physical transition but a financial one as well. Preparing adequately can make the difference between a smooth transition and a stressful one. Start by saving for a rental deposit, typically the first and last month's rent, well in advance. This deposit secures your tenancy and is usually refundable if you maintain the property well. Setting up utilities and internet might require initial fees or deposits, so inquire about these costs beforehand and include them in your moving budget.

Purchasing furniture and household items can also add up. Instead of buying everything new, consider economical options like second-hand stores, online marketplaces, or family hand-me-downs. Not only does this save money, but it also allows you to invest gradually in high-quality pieces over time. As you plan your move, create a checklist of essential items you'll need immediately —like a bed, a few kitchen supplies, and bathroom essentials—and then budget for additional items over the following months.

Remember, moving out is as much about managing your finances smartly as it is about creating a new home for yourself. By understanding and planning for the associated costs, creating a realistic budget, choosing the right housing, and preparing financially for the move, you equip yourself to survive and thrive in your new independence.

11.4 LONG-TERM FINANCIAL PLANNING: SETTING LIFE GOALS

Setting goals isn't just about deciding what you want to achieve; it's about mapping out a path that aligns with who you are and where you hope to be. When it comes to financial goals, employing the SMART criteria—Specific, Measurable, Achievable, Relevant, and Time-bound—transforms vague dreams into achievable milestones. Let's say you dream of owning a home. Instead of merely wishing for it, define what kind of home you want, research the cost, establish a savings plan, and set a timeline for achieving this goal. This method clarifies your path and embeds your financial pursuits deeply within your broader life aspirations, ensuring that every financial decision supports your values and long-term desires.

The journey through life is punctuated by significant events, each with financial implications. Whether pursuing higher education, planning a wedding, raising a family, buying your first home, or moving towards retirement, each life event requires thoughtful financial planning. For instance, funding higher education may involve exploring scholarships, grants, and student loans. Similarly, planning for a wedding may require setting aside savings monthly into a dedicated fund. As you look towards buying a home, understanding mortgage options becomes crucial. When thinking about retirement, early investments in retirement accounts can make the difference between merely surviving and thriving in your later years. The key is anticipating these events and planning early, allowing compound interest and careful investment to ease the financial burden when these milestones arrive.

In navigating the complexities of long-term financial planning, the guidance of a financial advisor can be invaluable. A financial advisor brings expertise in financial markets, investment strategies, and tax planning, which can enhance your ability to meet financial goals effectively. Their role becomes particularly crucial when you face major life decisions or transitions that involve substantial financial undertakings or when your financial situation becomes complex enough to benefit from professional management. For example, if you inherit assets or receive a large sum of money, a financial advisor can help you make decisions that optimize tax benefits and investment growth. They can also offer objective advice during emotionally charged times, such as a family estate settlement, ensuring decisions are made with a clear financial perspective.

Regular review and adjustment of your financial plan is not just beneficial; it's necessary. Your financial plan also needs to evolve as your life evolves—maybe you switch careers, move to a different city or experience changes in your family structure. This might mean adjusting your savings goals, reevaluating your investment portfolio, or modifying your insurance coverage. An annual review of your financial goals and instruments ensures that they continue to align with your current circumstances and future aspirations. It also allows you to respond to changes in the financial market and economic environment, securing your financial well-being against unforeseen challenges.

Navigating through these complexities might seem daunting, but remember, each decision you make builds towards a future where your financial stability allows you to live according to your values and dreams. As you close this chapter, reflect on the intertwining of your financial decisions with your personal growth and broader life goals. In the next chapter, we will explore how to maintain this alignment as you face new challenges and opportunities, ensuring that your financial strategy supports your journey through every stage of life.

CHAPTER TWELVE

STAYING MOTIVATED AND FINANCIALLY INFORMED

Imagine you're navigating a vast ocean, where waves of information constantly swirl around you. At times, it can feel overwhelming to stay afloat amidst the relentless surge of financial updates, market trends, and economic forecasts. This chapter is your compass and anchor, helping you navigate these waters confidently and clearly, ensuring you remain informed without getting overwhelmed. Our goal here is to keep you afloat and turn you into a skilled navigator of the financial seas, adept at using the tools and knowledge at your disposal to maintain your course toward financial literacy and independence.

12.1 KEEPING UP WITH FINANCIAL NEWS WITHOUT GETTING OVERWHELMED

Curate Your Sources

In the digital age, where information is abundant, the key to staying effectively informed is not about accessing more, but rather accessing better, more reliable information. Start by curating a list of renowned financial news sources for their credibility and quality. Look for publications and websites that provide financial news and do so in a balanced and understandable way. For instance, sources like "The Wall Street Journal," "Bloomberg," and "The Financial Times" are well-regarded for their thoroughness in financial reporting. However, these may be too dense for your current understanding.

To bridge this gap, consider turning to platforms geared specifically towards younger audiences or beginners in finance. Websites like Investopedia or Khan Academy offer explanations of complex financial concepts in simpler terms and can be excellent starting points. Furthermore, subscribing to newsletters from these sources can be a practical way to receive a curated digest of important financial news tailored to your interests and comprehension level.

Scheduled Updates

To avoid the fatigue that comes with constant exposure to financial news, it's crucial to set specific times for this activity. Designate a slot in your daily or weekly schedule dedicated solely to checking financial updates. This could be 30 minutes each morning or an hour over the weekend, depending on what suits your routine best. By confining your news-checking to these periods, you not only prevent the stress of constant notifications but also give yourself a structured time to absorb and reflect on the information.

There are also numerous apps and tools available that can help streamline this process. Apps like "Feedly" or "Flipboard" allow you to aggregate news from various sources into one platform, where you can customize your feeds to show only the topics you are interested in. This can significantly reduce the time you spend sifting through irrelevant information, making your learning more efficient and less overwhelming.

Understanding Financial Cycles

The financial world is inherently cyclical, with natural periods of growth and decline. Recognizing this can change how you perceive news of financial downturns or booms. Most importantly, it helps you understand that not every dip in the market signals disaster, nor does every peak promise lasting prosperity. These fluctuations are normal, and overreacting to them can be detrimental to your financial well-being.

To build this understanding, start by familiarizing yourself with the basic cycles of the economy—expansion, peak, contraction, and trough. Resources like economic textbooks, educational videos, or even financial podcasts can provide insights into these patterns. Knowing these cycles will help you contextualize the news you hear, enabling you to respond with informed calmness rather than reactive fear.

Critical Thinking Skills

As you grow more comfortable with financial terms and concepts, start to cultivate your critical thinking skills. Whenever you encounter a piece of financial news, take a moment to analyze it. Ask yourself: What is the source of this information? Is it presenting a fact, an opinion, or a prediction? What might be the motive behind this news piece? Is it trying to inform you, persuade you, or sell you something?

Also, always cross-reference news from multiple sources to verify its accuracy. This practice protects you from misinformation and deepens your understanding of how different events can be interpreted from various perspectives. Engaging critically with financial news in this way turns passive reading into active learning, enhancing your ability to make well-informed financial decisions.

By curating reliable sources, scheduling your news updates, understanding the cyclical nature of financial markets, and honing your critical thinking, you can transform the way you engage with financial news. This approach lets you stay informed and motivated without feeling overwhelmed by the vast seas of information, helping you navigate your financial goals confidently and clearly.

12.2 FINANCIAL PODCASTS AND BOOKS EVERY TEEN SHOULD KNOW ABOUT

Navigating the vast landscape of financial education can sometimes feel like searching for specific trees in an enormous forest. To help you find your way, I've curated a selection of podcasts and books tailored specifically for young audiences like yourself. These podcasts and books aim to transform complex financial concepts into engaging and digestible morsels of knowledge.

Let's start with podcasts, which are a fantastic way to dip your toes into the financial waters during your commute to school or while relaxing after a day's study. One notable podcast is "How to Money," hosted by Matt Altmix and Joel Larsgaard, which breaks down key financial concepts into manageable, teen-friendly episodes. They cover everything from basic budgeting to stock investing, making it ideal for beginners. Another great listen is "Teenager Financial Freedom," where young hosts discuss personal finance topics relevant to teenage listeners, including how to save money, ways to earn income, and tips for financial planning. These podcasts not only provide valuable insights but do so in a way that respects your growing independence and individual financial journeys.

Turning the page, let's talk about some essential reads that should be on every teen's bookshelf. "I Will Teach You to Be Rich" by Ramit Sethi is a great start. Don't let the title fool you; it's not about quick schemes but rather about smart, long-term financial habits. Sethi combines humor with practical advice, making it a relatable and enjoyable read. For those who are visual learners, "Rich Dad Poor Dad for Teens" by Robert T. Kiyosaki offers a graphic novel format, presenting financial lessons through engaging comic strips that illustrate complex concepts like investing and making money work for you.

Audiobooks and interactive books offer a wonderful alternative for those who find traditional books less engaging. Platforms like Audible provide access to a multitude of financial literacy books that you can listen to on the go. For a more interactive experience, "The Infographic Guide to Personal Finance" by Michele Cagan and Elisabeth Lariviere serves as a visual treat, presenting financial advice through bold infographics that make understanding money management both simple and fun.

Lastly, the idea of joining or starting a book club focused on financial topics can be incredibly enriching. Not only does it allow you to delve deeper into the material, but it also opens up a platform for discussion with peers who share your interests. This can be a safe space to express doubts, share successes, and gain diverse perspectives on money management. Schools, local libraries, or even online platforms can be ideal places to start such a club. Engaging collectively in these discussions can demystify the complexities of economics and personal finance, fostering a community of informed young investors and spenders who feel empowered to make smart financial decisions.

Through these resources—be it the solo journey of listening to a podcast, the shared experience of a book club, or the interactive process of an infographic book—you gain access to a wealth of knowledge tailored to help you confidently navigate your financial path. These tools are not just stepping stones but are part of a broader tapestry of resources that equip you with the skills to manage and grow your personal finances effectively as you move toward adulthood.

12.3 JOINING FINANCIALLY MINDED COMMUNITIES

The saying goes, "It takes a village," and this couldn't be truer when it comes to cultivating your financial literacy. Engaging with communities focused on financial education offers a treasure trove of benefits, from the shared wisdom of diverse experiences to the motivational boost that comes from belonging to a group with similar goals. Imagine walking into a virtual or physical room where everyone is eager to share what they've learned about managing money, investing, or saving. Here, questions are encouraged, successes are celebrated, and setbacks are seen as learning opportunities. This environment is not just about gaining knowledge; it's about experiencing the supportive energy that makes the financial learning journey less daunting and more doable.

When you decide to find your financial tribe, consider what resonates most with your personal interests and values. Start by exploring both online and offline options. Local community centers or schools often host clubs or workshops focused on financial education. These can provide a hands-on learning experience and the opportunity to meet peers in your area. On the other hand, online forums and social media platforms offer access to a global community where you can connect with financial experts and enthusiasts at any time. Platforms like Reddit have communities like r/personalfinance, which are goldmines of information and advice covering a wide range of topics. Similarly, platforms like Discord and Facebook host groups dedicated to specific aspects of finance, from basic budgeting to advanced investing.

When evaluating these communities, look for signs of active engagement, such as regular posts, thoughtful discussions, and respectful responses. Check if the information shared is generally reliable and supported by credible sources. It's also important to consider the community's culture. Does it foster a supportive and inclusive environment? Are there moderators or community guidelines in place to ensure discussions remain constructive and respectful? These factors significantly impact your learning experience, ensuring it is informative and enjoyable.

Once you've dipped your toes into various groups, you might feel inspired to start a finance club in your school or neighborhood. This can be a fantastic way to take a leadership role and tailor a learning experience that meets your peers' specific needs and interests. Begin by setting clear objectives for the club, such as improving members' financial literacy, preparing for college expenses, or learning about investing. Reach out to educators or community leaders who can provide guidance or support. They might help with resources, finding guest speakers, and organizing meetings.

Planning activities for the club should be both educational and engaging. Arrange workshops where members can learn to create and manage their budgets, invite financial advisors to talk about smart investing, or organize simulations of stock market trading. Consider community service projects, like offering basic financial education to younger students, which can reinforce your learning and benefit others. These activities enhance understanding of financial concepts and strengthen community bonds, making the learning process a shared, communal journey.

By actively participating in or leading a financially minded community, you expand your knowledge and develop essential life skills such as communication, leadership, and critical thinking. More importantly, you'll find that being part of such a community can transform the often-intimidating world of finance into an accessible and even enjoyable part of your life.

12.4 SETTING AND REVIEWING FINANCIAL GOALS AS YOU GROW

Imagine your life as a series of stepping stones across a river. Each stone represents a goal, and while some are closer and smaller, others are further away and larger. These represent the short-term and long-term aspirations that guide your journey. Establishing a structured framework for setting these financial goals is like mapping out a path across the river, ensuring each step is thoughtfully placed to support your journey toward financial independence.

Start by categorizing your goals into short-term, medium-term, and long-term. Short-term goals are those you hope to achieve within the next year or two, like saving for a new laptop or funding a summer road trip with friends. Medium-term goals might span two to five years, including saving for a car or starting a college fund. Long-term goals stretch beyond five years and often involve larger financial commitments, such as saving for a down payment on a house or planning for retirement, even if it seems a lifetime away.

As life flows on, your financial and personal situation will inevitably evolve. Perhaps you'll start a new job with a higher salary or face unexpected expenses that strain your budget. These changes mean your initial set of goals might no longer align with your current reality. This is why it's crucial to review your goals at least annually. This regular check-in is your chance to adjust your plans based on new information or changes in your circumstances, ensuring your financial strategies remain responsive and relevant. During these reviews, ask yourself whether your goals are still attainable, if they continue to reflect your values, and how external factors like economic changes might influence your plans.

Visualization tools can be incredibly powerful in keeping your financial goals clear and focused. Visualizing success is like creating a personal map where each goal is a landmark. Use tools like charts, which can graphically represent your savings and spending in various categories, helping you see where you are on your financial path. Vision boards can also be a fun and inspiring way to keep your goals in sight. By creating a physical or digital collage of images and phrases that represent your goals, you anchor your aspirations in reality. Apps like Credit Karma or YNAB offer digital dashboards that integrate your financial data, allowing you to track your progress in real-time and adjust your course as needed.

Celebrating milestones is essential. Every goal reached is a triumph, whether it's small, like saving enough for a new game, or large, like funding your first semester at college. Create a ritual or establish a reward system that acknowledges these achievements. This might be as simple as a night out with friends or something more symbolic, like adding a photo to your vision board. Celebrating reinforces positive financial behaviors and boosts your morale, reminding you that your efforts have tangible rewards.

This structured approach to setting and reviewing your goals, paired with visual tools and celebrations, transforms the abstract concept of financial planning into a dynamic and interactive part of your life. It encourages a proactive attitude towards money management, making the process of financial growth both rewarding and instructive.

As this chapter closes, remember that setting and reviewing your financial goals is not just about planning for the future. It's about creating a responsive and personalized roadmap that evolves with you, reflecting your values, aspirations, and the inevitable changes life brings. This process is essential to building a financially secure and fulfilling life. As we transition into the next chapter, we'll explore how to apply these strategies in real-world scenarios, ensuring that you're well-prepared to meet future financial challenges and equipped to take advantage of opportunities that come your way.

KEEPING THE KNOWLEDGE FLOWING

Now you have everything you need to achieve financial independence, it's time to pass on your newfound knowledge and show other readers where they can find the same help.

Simply by leaving your honest opinion of this book on Amazon, you'll show other teens where they can find the information they're looking for, and pass their passion for personal finance forward.

Thank you for your help. *Personal Finance for Teens* is kept alive when we pass on our knowledge – and you're helping me to do just that.

Simply scan the QR code below to leave your review:

CONCLUSION

As we wrap up our journey through the pages of this guide, it's important to revisit the essence of why we embarked on this path together. Our main objective was clear from the start: to empower you, the teens of today, with the knowledge and tools necessary for financial literacy and independence. From the basics of budgeting to the complexities of investing, and the careful use of credit, we've covered a broad spectrum of topics, all aimed at transforming you from a financially uncertain teen into a confident, financially savvy young adult.

Throughout this book, we've delved into essential financial concepts such as creating your first budget, the magic of compound interest in savings, the strategic thinking behind investing, and the wise use of credit. We've discussed the importance of starting early with your financial planning, emphasizing that the sooner you begin, the more you can benefit from your financial decisions.

One of the core themes we've explored is the importance of ethical and responsible finance. It's crucial to recognize that your financial decisions have the power to impact your life and the world around you. By engaging in socially responsible investing or making ethical and sustainable purchases, you contribute to a positive change in society and the environment.

The world of finance is ever-evolving, and so should your knowledge and understanding of it. Please continue educating yourself and staying informed about new financial tools, economic changes, and marketplace shifts. This ongoing engagement with financial matters will equip you to navigate the complexities of the financial world as it changes.

Now, I urge you to take action. Whether it's drafting a simple budget, opening a savings account, or initiating a conversation about finances with your family and/or guardians, every small step counts. Begin today, and remember, the path to financial independence isn't about perfection; it's about progression.

It's natural to encounter setbacks and make mistakes along your financial journey. Instead of letting these challenges discourage you, view them as valuable learning experiences. Each setback is an opportunity to grow stronger and become more adept at managing your finances.

Remember, achieving financial independence is not a distant dream; it's a realistic and attainable goal. With the right information, tools, and a proactive approach, you can set yourself on a path to a secure and prosperous future.

I invite you to share your financial journey with others—celebrate your successes and discuss your challenges. By sharing your experiences, you help build a supportive community of young individuals who are passionate about growing their financial literacy.

Looking ahead, I envision a future where you, today's teens, become tomorrow's financially astute adults. You are the pioneers of wise financial decision-making, leading by example and paving the way for a future that is prosperous for yourselves and benevolent towards the world around you.

Let's continue supporting each other, learning continuously, and confidently leading. Here's to your success on this incredible journey towards financial independence and beyond!

REFERENCES

Banzai. (n.d.). Retrieved July 3, 2024, from https://banzai.org/courses/finlit/middle-school

Better Money Habits. (n.d.). Budgeting tips for teens in 6 easy steps. Retrieved July 3, 2024, from https://bettermoneyhabits.bankofamerica.com/en/personal-banking/teaching-children-how-to-budget

Big Life Journal. (n.d.). How to help teens set effective goals (tips & templates). Retrieved July 3, 2024, from https://biglifejournal.com/blogs/blog/guide-effective-goal-setting-teens-template-worksheet

CBS News. (2024). Top 3 online scams teens and parents should know about plus how to avoid them. Retrieved July 3, 2024, from https://www.cbsnews.com/newyork/news/top-3-online-scams-teens-and-parents-should-know-about-plus-how-to-avoid-them/

Consumer Credit. (n.d.). Youth and money archives. Retrieved July 3, 2024, from https://www.consumercredit.com/debt-resources-tools/youth-money/

CreditDonkey. (2024). 9 best stock market simulators for practice your skills 2024. Retrieved July 3, 2024, from https://www.creditdonkey.com/best-stock-market-simulators.html

DFPI. (2024). Three steps to managing and getting out of debt. Retrieved July 3, 2024, from https://dfpi.ca.gov/2024/04/23/three-steps-to-managing-and-getting-out-of-debt/#:.

Experian. (n.d.). 8 ways to help your teen build good credit now. Retrieved July 3, 2024, from https://www.experian.com/blogs/ask-experian/how-to-help-your-teen-build-credit/

Experian. (n.d.). Good debt vs. bad debt: What's the difference? Retrieved July 3, 2024, from https://www.experian.com/blogs/ask-experian/good-debt-vs-bad-debt-whats-the-difference/

Experian. (n.d.). The complete guide to understanding credit scores. Retrieved July 3, 2024, from https://www.experian.com/blogs/ask-experian/credit-education/score-basics/understanding-credit-scores/

FamZoo. (n.d.). Retrieved July 3, 2024, from https://famzoo.com/

Finance Monthly. (2023). A beginner's guide to using investing apps for financial growth. Retrieved July 3, 2024, from https://www.finance-monthly.com/2023/06/a-beginners-guide-to-using-investing-apps-for-financial-growth/

Financial Football. (n.d.). Retrieved July 3, 2024, from https://www.financialfootbal
l.com/

Financial Soccer. (n.d.). Retrieved July 3, 2024, from https://financialsoccer.com/en

Forbes Finance Council. (2020). 13 tips to help protect your online financial information. Retrieved July 3, 2024, from https://www.forbes.com/sites/forbesfi
nancecouncil/2020/04/27/13-tips-to-help-protect-your-online-financial-
information/

GoHenry. (n.d.). What is compound interest? Explaining to kids and teens.
Retrieved July 3, 2024, from https://www.gohenry.com/us/blog/financial-
education/what-is-compound-interest-explaining-to-kids-and-teens

IdentityTheft.gov. (n.d.). Retrieved July 3, 2024, from https://www.identitytheft.
gov/

Indeed. (n.d.). 11 job interview tips for teens. Retrieved July 3, 2024, from https://
www.indeed.com/career-advice/interviewing/interview-tips-for-teens

Intrepid Eagle Finance. (n.d.). The guide to Roth IRAs for teenagers. Retrieved July
3, 2024, from https://intrepideaglefinance.com/blog/the-guide-to-roth-iras-
for-teenagers

Investopedia. (n.d.). Investing for teens: What they should know. Retrieved July 3,
2024, from https://www.investopedia.com/investing-for-teens-7111843

Investopedia. (n.d.). Negotiation: Stages and strategies. Retrieved July 3, 2024, from
https://www.investopedia.com/terms/n/negotiation.asp

Investopedia. (n.d.). Return on investment meaning and calculation formulas.
Retrieved July 3, 2024, from https://www.investopedia.com/articles/basics/10/
guide-to-calculating-roi.asp

Investopedia. (n.d.). The importance of diversification. Retrieved July 3, 2024, from
https://www.investopedia.com/investing/importance-diversification/

Investopedia. (n.d.). The power of compound interest: Calculations and examples.
Retrieved July 3, 2024, from https://www.investopedia.com/terms/c/
compoundinterest.asp

Investopedia. (n.d.). Understanding purchasing power and the consumer price
index. Retrieved July 3, 2024, from https://www.investopedia.com/terms/p/
purchasingpower.asp

Jump Gap Software. (n.d.). iAllowance app (Apple) – allowance (can be based on
chores and/or auto-deposit). Retrieved July 3, 2024, from https://www.jumpgap
software.com/allowance/index.html

Junior Achievement USA. (n.d.). *JA teen budgeting: Income and spending worksheets.*
Retrieved from https://jausa.ja.org/programs/supplements/ja-teen-budgeting-
income-and-spending-worksheets

KidsMoney.org. (n.d.). 23 best money apps for teens. Retrieved July 3, 2024, from
https://www.kidsmoney.org/teens/money-management/apps/

KidsMoney.org. (n.d.). Best budgeting apps for teens (I tried them all). Retrieved July 3, 2024, from https://www.kidsmoney.org/teens/budgeting/apps/

LSS Financial Counseling. (n.d.). Alternatives to student loans [reduce higher education costs]. Retrieved July 3, 2024, from https://www.lssmn.org/financial counseling/blog/alternatives-student-loans-reduce-higher-education-costs

Money Management International. (n.d.). How to master the art of comparison shopping. Retrieved July 3, 2024, from https://www.moneymanagement.org/blog/comparison-shopping

MyDoh. (n.d.). Best budgeting apps and calculators for kids and teens. Retrieved July 3, 2024, from https://www.mydoh.ca/learn/money-101/money-basics/best-budgeting-apps-and-calculators-for-kids-and-teens/

MyDoh. (n.d.). Emergency funds explained for teens. Retrieved July 3, 2024, from https://www.mydoh.ca/learn/money-101/building-credit/emergency-funds-explained-for-teens/

MyDoh. (n.d.). How to help kids and teens avoid impulse buying. Retrieved July 3, 2024, from https://www.mydoh.ca/learn/blog/lifestyle/how-to-help-kids-and-teens-avoid-impulse-buying/

Navy Federal Credit Union. (n.d.). 6 credit card tips to teach your teen. Retrieved July 3, 2024, from https://www.navyfederal.org/makingcents/credit-debt/teen-credit-card-tips.html

NerdWallet. (n.d.). 10 best banking apps and debit cards for kids and teens. Retrieved July 3, 2024, from https://www.nerdwallet.com/article/banking/buzzy-banking-apps-for-kids-and-teens

Oxford Royale. (n.d.). 14 teen entrepreneurs and how they succeeded. Retrieved July 3, 2024, from https://www.oxford-royale.com/articles/14-teen-entrepreneurs/

Practical Money Skills. (n.d.). Retrieved July 3, 2024, from https://www.practicalmoneyskills.com/en/play/payoff.html

Ramsey Solutions. (2022). How to read a credit card statement. Retrieved July 3, 2024, from https://www.ramseysolutions.com/debt/reading-your-credit-card-statement

Regions. (n.d.). Budgeting for teens: Teaching teens to save. Retrieved July 3, 2024, from https://www.regions.com/insights/personal/personal-finances/budgeting-and-saving/teaching-teens-how-to-save-money

RoosterMoney. (n.d.). Retrieved July 3, 2024, from https://roostermoney.com/

Schwab Moneywise. (n.d.). Helping teens use credit wisely. Retrieved July 3, 2024, from https://www.schwabmoneywise.com/teaching-kids/using-credit-wisely

Schwab Moneywise. (n.d.). Moneywise America | Financial literacy for teens. Retrieved July 3, 2024, from https://www.schwabmoneywise.com/moneywise-america

Schwab. (n.d.). How to read stock charts and trading patterns. Retrieved July 3, 2024, from https://www.schwab.com/learn/story/how-to-read-stock-charts-and-trading-patterns

Schwab. (n.d.). SMART goals for your financial plan. Retrieved July 3, 2024, from https://www.schwab.com/learn/story/smart-goals-your-financial-plan

Step. (n.d.). Retrieved July 3, 2024, from https://step.com/

TaxSlayer. (n.d.). Do teens have to file taxes? A beginner's guide. Retrieved July 3, 2024, from https://www.taxslayer.com/blog/teen-filing-first-tax-return/

The Guardian. (2006). Peer pressure forces young adults to spend, says report. Retrieved July 3, 2024, from https://www.theguardian.com/money/2006/dec/13/retail.business

U.S. Department of Labor. (n.d.). YouthRules. Retrieved July 3, 2024, from https://www.dol.gov/agencies/whd/youthrules

U.S. Internal Revenue Service. (n.d.). Common tax return mistakes that can cost taxpayers. Retrieved July 3, 2024, from https://www.irs.gov/newsroom/common-tax-return-mistakes-that-can-cost-taxpayers

U.S. Internal Revenue Service. (n.d.). Education credits AOTC LLC. Retrieved July 3, 2024, from https://www.irs.gov/credits-deductions/individuals/education-credits-aotc-llc

U.S. Internal Revenue Service. (n.d.). File your taxes for free. Retrieved July 3, 2024, from https://www.irs.gov/filing/free-file-do-your-federal-taxes-for-free

Washington State Department of Financial Institutions. (n.d.). Financial education at home: Grades 9-12. Retrieved from https://dfi.wa.gov/financial-education/at-home/grades-9-12

World of Money. (n.d.). Retrieved July 3, 2024, from https://www.worldofmoney.org/